Peter

Thank you for a good evening
& good company!

Best wishes

Jeremy AR

75 YEARS
OF BALLS

IMPERIAL POONA YACHT CLUB

75 YEARS
OF BALLS

THE HISTORY OF THE

IMPERIAL POONA
YACHT CLUB

By The Gully Gully Man

(A.K.A. Jeremy Atkins)

FORWARD

BUCKINGHAM PALACE.

It is undoubtedly true that life is a serious business, but that does not mean that it has to be taken seriously all the time. The Imperial Poona (Pune – in newspeak) Yacht Club is, in many senses of the word, a standard yacht club, but it is also, what might be termed, an anti-yacht club, founded by the arch anti-serious hero, Reginald Bennett.

I am delighted that the Gully Gully Man has undertaken to compose an account of the club's first 75 years. I believe that he has successfully met the challenge to combine historical accuracy while contending with the outrageous and the absurd. It is true that all the members are serious yachtsmen, in the sense that they are all rather good at it, but, what is equally important is that they all share a keen appreciation of the value of anti-seriousness. If you can bring yourself to read this book from cover to cover, you will be in a position to judge for yourself whether, or not, life can be significantly improved by not taking it too seriously all the time.

The Maharajah of Cooch Parwani

SIR REGINALD BENNETT, V.R.D.
(1911 – 2000)

It is only appropriate to start with the Club's leading light. The following obituary, written by John Barnes, appeared in The Independent on 28th December 2000 and is reprinted by kind permission of The Independent, Obituaries.

Reginald Bennett was a psychiatrist by profession, a yachtsman who represented Britain in international races against America and was unlucky never to take part in the Olympics, a long-serving Conservative MP and a thoroughly nice man.

His penetrating intellect and popularity in the House should have secured him a ministerial post but, at a time when MPs were expected to take life and themselves seriously, his inability to conform denied him the chance that he richly deserved. Had Iain Macleod lived, it is more than possible that Bennett, whom he understood well, might have found a place in the Government's ranks. But in reality it was too late. It was said that his prowess as a helmsman did him no favours with Heath, but his whole style was out of keeping with that of his leader and, just as he backed Macleod, until the latter dropped out of the leadership race, he would have felt far more at home in a party led by Reggie Maudling.

As one of his opponents, Tam Dalyell, observes, "There is an awful temptation for people to become caricatures of themselves in the House of Commons and he rather played at being the bon viveur to the extent that it damaged his chances of being taken seriously." Later entries in Dod's Parliamentary Companion solemnly record him as Chevalier du Tastevin 1971, de St Etienne (Alsace) 1972, de Bretvin (Muscadet) 1973, Commander de Bontemps-Medoc 1959. That tells its own tale. But in addition to chairing the Catering sub-committee of the House of Commons Services Committee from 1970 to 1974, he had chaired the Parliamentary Scientific Committee from 1958 to 1962, and that too should be remarked.

Born in Sheffield in 1911, the son of a civil servant, Reggie Bennett won scholarships to both Winchester and New College, Oxford, where he read Physiology, before completing his medical training in London at St George's Hospital and the Maudsley. It was his proud boast that he had qualified as a pilot in the University Air Squadron before he learnt to drive a car and he subsequently joined the London Division of the Royal Naval Volunteer Reserve. As a Surgeon Lieutenant-Commander he served first in Western Approaches and then with the Northern Patrol. He twice survived being torpedoed. He gained his wings with the Fleet Air Arm in 1941 and served first in Tanganyika and then in Ceylon. He was awarded the Volunteer Reserve Decoration in 1944.

At Oxford he had been awarded his Blue for sailing for each year from 1931 until 1934, the year in which he sailed for Britain against Germany at the Kiel Regatta and won the City of Hamburg Cup. In 1934 and 1935 he took the helm of Sir Richard Fairey's J-Class yacht Shamrock V in the races against the United States, but was reserve for the 1936 Olympics. Had the Second World War not intervened it is likely that he would have taken part in the 1940 Olympics. From 1936 until 1938 he raced the 12-metre Evaine and, after the War, represented Britain in the British-American Cup races in 1949 and 1953. By then he was a Conservative MP and helped found the House of Commons Yacht Club, eventually serving as its Commodore.

He had been adopted for Woolwich East in 1937 and had contested it unsuccessfully in 1945. He was elected for Gosport and Fareham in 1950 and continued to represent the seat until it was divided. From February 1974 until he retired from the Commons in 1979 he represented Fareham. He served as Parliamentary Private Secretary to the Home Secretary from 1951 until 1954 and to the Minister of Fuel and Power, 1954-55, before being invited by Iain Macleod to become his PPS in 1955. "As someone who's had two ministers shot from under you," Macleod scribbled, "I wonder if you would consider coming and looking after me."

The two had met in the late 1940s when Macleod was at the Conservative Research Department and Bennett had offered to brief the party on health. Fond, some would say excessively so, of the camaraderie and gossip of the smoking room, he proved to be an ideal pair of ears and eyes for his minister, not least when Macleod was in deep trouble with the right of his party as Colonial Secretary from 1959 to 1961.

A shrewd judge of fellow Members, he warned Macleod during the leadership contest in 1963 that the choice would fall on the Foreign Secretary, Lord Home. According to Bennett, this news was greeted with total disbelief, but nevertheless in the early hours of 12 October, with Bennett serving "long thin scotches", Macleod briefed two of the leading political correspondents that Home was in the running. Bennett would never say, and may not have known, whether this was part of a bid to stall the leading candidates in mid-fight, so enabling a younger candidate to come through.

In the end, "quixotically" in Bennett's opinion, Macleod told Home to his face why he should not be Prime Minister and, unable to serve, retired to the back benches. Had he run in 1965, Bennett would have been among those organising his candidature, but his public denunciation of the "magic circle" that had picked Home had denied him any chance of victory.

It was at Bennett's invitation that Macleod joined the Thursday Club, which met over lunch at Wheeler's Restaurant in Soho to drink Chablis and establish the proposition that the weekend was about to begin. Later this involved the so-called Wessex Hunting Club, an occasion for foolery and hard drinking. Prince Philip was a member of the Thursday Club and was later invited to join the Imperial Poona Yacht Club, founded by Bennett when at Oxford for the purpose of challenging current undergraduates to take part in a backwards sailing race down the Thames.

There was a more serious side to him. As a young MP he became a member of the Inner Temple and took a great interest in the affairs of the Medico-Legal Society. He spoke several languages including Arabic, Swahili and Italian, and chaired the Anglo-Italian Parliamentary Group for nine years. He wrote "Why Executives Die Young" in 1953 and "Psychological Disturbances of Young Married Life" in 1954 as well as medical pamphlets. He took an interest in polio research and the effect of polluted seawater, making the memorable comment that swimming in the Solent was "not so much swimming as going through the motions".

Three years ago he published a memoir, "Three Chousing Reers".

THE CONTEXT

The earnest endeavour of the founders of the Oxford & Cambridge Sailing Society, recounted in the other part of this volume shows an enthusiastic, but perhaps somewhat arrogant attitude (inviting themselves to sail other people's boats) which was present at Oxbridge in the 1930s.

These were the early years of Brideshead Revisited – the time when Charles Ryder first met Sebastian Flyte at Oxford – the First World War a fading memory and no thought of another European conflict. Britain ruled the waves and the sun never set on the Empire.

A posting in India was common for many a profession, whether it be soldier, policeman, civil servant or whatever. In India, the British lived a privileged existence, and some found it hard to return to Blighty and settle back into a less exotic life. And, perhaps after too much time in the sun, they just wished to tell everyone they met about life in India.

Sir Reginald Bennett paints the picture in his memoir 'Three Chousing Reers':

In those days England was full of retired bigwigs from the Indian Army, the Civil Service and so forth who all reminisced at length. A chap called Sir Archie Hope of Balliol, the 17th Baronet, ... was up in North Berwick, where he lived, one Christmas vacation and he went to a Hunt Ball. He was bored absolutely sick by these old-timers going on and on. One he quoted as being really the most fantastically boring, was an old boy who kept haranguing him about the fishing customs of the hill tribes of the Brahmaputra. We thought that was quite absurd. The only way to cope with this was to start talking the same language back at such people, and so we founded this Club, based on the theme: "When I was in Poona ..."

This was the context for the Imperial Poona Yacht Club – it was a reaction against the Imperial bores of the day, and saw its role as making fun of them and their attitudes, using their language. As stated in the historical notes in the Club's handbook: "*It had been felt that a club embodying something of the Anglo-Indian culture was needed. The Club should regard Imperial Thinking as paramount.*"

The language is of those who are being mocked and is not to be taken seriously, but accepted for what it is – in modern parlance – a piss-take on the Imperial attitudes of the time.

If this is not understood, and the language taken seriously, the point will be missed.

Equally well, if the Imperial Poona Yacht Club ever takes itself seriously, it will have failed its founders.

THE FIRST INCARNATION

The Foundation

Somewhat surprisingly, for a Club which was set up on almost anti-establishment lines, a Minute Book was maintained up to the 1950s. It records:

The Imperial Poona Yacht Club was founded on Sunday, April 22nd, 1934 on the banks of the River Thames at Abingdon, the station of the Oxford University Yacht Club. During the Sunday afternoon's racing in which R.F.B. Bennett, then Vice Commodore of the O.U.Y.C., and A.W.A. Whitehead were taking part, there arrived Sir Archibald Hope, Baronet, and Charlie H. Johnston. They were expressing themselves in Anglo Indian terminology. These suggested the formation of a limited club on Anglo Indian lines, and there appeared to be three good reasons for its formation.

1. Experiences, of those present, with Anglo Indians, culminating perhaps in information given recently to Sir Archibald Hope on the subject of the Fishing Customs of the Hill Tribes of the Brahmaputra.

2. The need for an association to knit together the small but diffuse collection of people who had in recent years, in their various permutations and combinations, been at the back of much party-making.

3. The desirability of some society to collect keen young sailing men, often but not always from the Universities, without the rather unjustified premises on which the Oxford and Cambridge Sailing Society had been founded.

The Oxford & Cambridge Sailing Society had been formed on 24th February 1934, but Reggie Bennett had not been invited to be a member. On the face of it, this was surprising given that he had sailed for Oxford in the Varsity Match since 1931, and was the Vice Commodore (senior undergraduate) of the OUYC, but Reggie and Stewart Morris (the Society's leading light) never got on. Reggie may have been using Anglo Indian terminology to mock those returning from India, but he was also making fun of Stewart and his Society.

One can perhaps see some of Reggie's mischief-making in evidence in the report in the other history in this volume that "*the Society's founding meeting heard that 'certain people' from the Royal Corinthian Yacht Club* [where Reggie was known to sail] *considered it* [the Oxford & Cambridge Sailing Society] *a name to which the persons present had no claim – it would not be representative of either Oxford or*

Cambridge." Reggie uses rather similar language when referring to the Society's "*rather unjustified premises*".

Given the largely similar nursery for the two organisations, it is interesting to note that, Henry Trefusis, a friend of Reggie's at school and Oxford, was the only founding member of both clubs.

Two of Poona's other early members were later elected to the Society – Richard Webster in 1936 and John Palmer in 1938, so membership of the two Clubs did overlap, but only very slightly in the initial years.

The Rules & Constitution

The four present, on the banks of the Thames, when the momentous decision to form the Club was made, proceeded that evening to formulate a constitution and draw up the Club's rules:

It was decided to found the Club on Poona, that name so dear to the Anglo Indian. And it was considered good that the Club should be a yacht club. The prefix 'Imperial' was chosen to avoid confusion with clubs which held a Royal warrant. The Club was therefore named the Imperial Poona Yacht Club.

It must have been a good evening, because the set of rules they produced have largely remained unaltered, and still provide amusement when one appreciates how firmly their tongues were placed in their cheeks.

Membership was limited to fifteen '*Pukkah Sahibs*', who had to be unmarried men. While the title of Commodore was traditional (although the holder is more usually referred to as The Commode), there were to be no Vice or Rear Commodores – instead they were the Great White Vice and Great Gorgeous Rear. All members were given appropriate Anglo Indian names.

The original rules and constitution read as follows:

IMPERIAL POONA YACHT CLUB
RULES AND CONSTITUTION

1. **The Club** shall be known as the Imperial Poona Yacht Club.
2. **The Objects of the Club** shall be
   (a) To promote Imperial Feeling.
   (b) To promote Team Sailing in Imperial Waters.
   (c) To promote Coloured Races among all Recognised Yacht Clubs within the British Empire.

3. **The Station of the Club**.
   The Club will have no particular station other than the British Empire.
4. **Politics**.
   The Club will be non-political, all members being pledged to an Imperial Party.
5. **Membership**.
   Membership shall be limited to 15, all of whom must be Pukka Sahibs, members of Recognised Yacht Clubs within the British Empire, and unmarried British Subjects. No memsahibs are eligible.
6. **Election to Membership**.
   A candidate for election must be vouched for in writing to the Secretariat-Wallah by no less than 4 (four) members to whom he is personally known. The Secretariat-Wallah shall then circularise all members, and if two black topees are received within a month the candidature will lapse. Otherwise the candidate shall be considered elected.
7. **Entrance Fee**.
   There shall be an entrance fee of 64 (sixty-four) sixty-fourths (64ths) of a rupee, payable on election to membership.
8. **Cessation of Membership**.
   Membership shall terminate automatically on
   (a) Marriage.
   (b) Death.
   (c) Ceasing to be a member of a Recognised Yacht Club within the British Empire.
   (d) Bankruptcy, unless otherwise authorised by the Club.
   (e) Temporarily, on imprisonment or deportation.
9. **Marriage**.
   Any member contracting a marriage shall stand a dinner to all the other members of the Club, who shall retaliate, if desired, with a guard of honour.
10. **Officers**.
    The Officers of the Club shall consist of: a Commodore, a Great White Vice, a Great Gorgeous Rear, a Secretariat-Wallah, a Finance Member, an Honorary Chaplain (who shall be the then Archbishop of Poona if the said Archbishop of Poona be a member of a Recognised Yacht Club within the British Empire, not legally married, etc., etc.), a serang, a crackswain, a shanty-muezzin, a donkeyman, a punkah-wallah, a currie-fellah, and any others that may hereafter be instituted.

11. **Committee**.
The Committee shall consist of the officers together with the other members.

12. **Commodore**.
The Commodore shall be chosen for his ability and experience in handling Coloured Races.

13. **Tiffin**.
An annual Tiffin shall be held whenever circumstances require, and at it the toast of "Poona" shall always be drunk.

14. **Quorum**.
Four or more members may constitute a Tiffin.

15. **Chair**.
At Tiffin the senior officer present shall take the chair.

16. **Speeches**.
At Tiffin every member present must make a speech.

17. **Bhoi**.
If at Tiffin the Hon. Haro-Bhoi be present the Ceremonies of Foulin and Roundin the Bhoi shall be gone through.

18. **Class**.
The Club shall sail for preference in the Brahmaputra Restricted or Swettipore One-Design Class (hereinafter referred to as the S.O.D.'s). Any class may be so designated for the time being, and failing this a class shall be constituted with not less than one design per boat.

19. **Motto**.
The Motto of the Club shall be "Chota Hazri."

20. **Insignia**.
The Club tie and Burgee may be obtainable at Messrs. W.H. Walker's, The Broad, Oxford.

21. **Finance**.
A statement of accounts shall be issued by the Secretariat-Wallah or Finance Member or both.

22. **Alteration of Rules**.
Any rule may be altered on notice to the Secretariat-Wallah and circularization by him, provided that 2/3 (two thirds) of the members agree to the proposed alteration.

23. **Resignation Forms**.
Resignation forms may always be obtained from the Hon. Chaplain Sahib, provided that sufficient notice be given.

The Club's motto of *"Chota Hazri"*, was once translated by Reggie as *"There is nothing worse than a continental breakfast"*. According to Jyotsna Shahane on her website, thecookscottage, it actually refers to *"a little brekker of tea and biscuits, usually served in the bedroom, in a propah tea set dedicated to the purpose. This was followed somewhat later by a pukka larger breakfast.*" (Used with kind permission: http://thecookscottage.typepad.com).

Initial Members & Inaugural Tiffin

The foundation members are recorded in the Minute Book as:

Sir Archibald Hope, Bt	Commodore
C.H. Johnston	Great White Vice
J.F.R. Mitchell	Great Gorgeous Rear
R.F.B. Bennett	Chaplain
A.W.A. Whitehead	Secretariat Wallah
J.H.M. Rabone	Punkah Wallah

With the following also elected immediately:

Henry Trefusis	Shanty-Muezzin
P.J. Norton	Ayah
T.C. Maples	Acting Haro-Bhoi
P.P. Powell	Haro-Bhoi & Donkeyman
J.C.L. Palmer	Serang

And the numbers bought up to the full fifteen the following month:

F.O.S Dobell	Irrigation Fellah
R.N. Webster	Untouchable
Squadron Leader W.A.K. Dalzell	Currie Fellah
Flight Officer G.K. Fairtlough	Djinn

Some of this membership reflects Reggie's other love at the time – flying, which was also the subject of an incident early on in the Club's history:

Shortly after the inception of the Club, the Commodore and Chaplain were submitted to an aerial attack by an Auro Lynx SO4N, containing F/O G.K. Fairtlough, RAF, and Mr P.C. Wheeler, OUAS. This aircraft then proceeded to traverse some telephone wires over the river, removing them en route. Justification was pleaded on the grounds that, in the course of many miles flown over many kinds of water in the Fleet Air Arm, the pilot had never encountered wire before.

Purportedly as a result of this incident, Fairtlough was "*posted away on the grounds of 'unsuitability (temperamental) for instructing undergraduates'.*"

12

However, as luck would have it, the Club's inaugural Tiffin coincided with this and so doubled up as his Farewell Tiffin, which was held at the Oxford University Air Squadron, Manor Road on 11th May 1934. Seven members were present and five other guests. Although not of very good quality, the photo of this very first Tiffin has to be included.

The Imperial Poona Yacht Club's First Tiffin, 11th May, 1934

There were multiple speeches, various performances, climbing of the flag posts and moving of vehicles. But the echoes of Brideshead Revisted are clear in the account of what happened to the unfortunate Philip Wheeler who was a guest (and probably still recovering from his earlier flight):

Mr Wheeler toured Oxford on an unlit bicycle, twice circulating the Clarendon Garage at high speed before being apprehended by a policeman standing 'like Christ crucified' in the gateway. He proceeded to mislead the policeman and made an unsuccessful attempt to escape. Being bailed out by the Proctors [University officials]*, his whole misdeeds were laid bare and he was, after an angry scene with the Dean of New College, sent down, the first Poona martyr.*

Probably as a result of this performance, he was elected a member in October 1934.

His election was possible because two members had left the Club. P.P. Powell was *"deported and made Hon. Canadian Representative. Later to be engaged to be married."* And J.H.M. Rabone was, more mysteriously, *"required to resign through non-fulfilment of conditions of membership."* (Apparently he had ceased to be a member of a recognised yacht club).

If individuals did not meet the Club's strict criteria (usually because they were married), but were felt to behave sufficiently imperially, they were elected to Honorary membership, as was the case for F.G. Mitchell (Honorary Colonel in Chief) and Colin Ratsey (Honorary Sails Manager).

Further Tiffins

The Minute Book records eleven further Tiffins which were held in 1934:

14th July	Royal Corinthian Yacht Club, Burnham
18th July	Officers' Mess, RAF Eastchurch, Kent
20th July	Officers' Mess, RAF Eastchurch, Kent
26th July	On board 'Eclipse' at Newhaven
28th July	On board 'Eclipse' at Cowes (this Tiffin *"continued for several days!"*)
1st – 8th September	During Burnham Week (*"throughout the week the toast of Poona was drunk"*).
10th October	The Aerodrome Hotel, Croydon
10th November	At Oxford, under the auspices of OUYC
22nd November	Royal Thames Yacht Club, Knightsbridge
24th November	Burnham-on-Crouch
30th November	101 Piccadilly and the Running Horse hostelry

These appear to have been a variety of informal events which took place whenever at least four members of the Club (as required by the Constitution) gathered together. While not strictly a flag officer of the Club, it was clear who was the driving force behind all of them – the only person present at all twelve Tiffins in 1934 – Reggie Bennett!

Sailing

But it would be wrong to suppose that Poona's only activity in its first year was at Tiffins.

Roy Mitchell and Reggie Bennett represented England in the Twelve Square Metre International Sharpie Class at Kiel. *"Against the most strenuous opposition from Germany, Holland and Switzerland, and*

*less strenuous from Sweden, Italy, Finland and Poland, the results showed
England first with five wins and one second in six races."*

At Cowes, five members of the Oxford University Varsity Match team were Poona members, and the sixth (David Wilson) was subsequently elected. Unfortunately they failed to achieve victory over the Tabs, and a draw was declared.

In America, Roy Mitchell and Colin Ratsey represented the Club on board 'Endeavour' challenging for the Americas Cup. Meanwhile, in the UK, Reggie and John Palmer sailed on board another J Class yacht, 'Shamrock V', for a month, with a record of *"4 (or 5) firsts and 7 seconds in 16 races."*

Insignia

The Club's tie was designed to be worn with Morning Dress by the guard of honour when a member resigned through matrimony, and had already been used for such a purpose within six months of the foundation of the Club. It had a silver-grey background, with red topees.

The burgee similarly had a red topee, but this time on a yellow background. (The famous red balls were only introduced after the War).

Gillie Potter also designed a yachting cap badge for the Club during Burnham Week, some of which are still in the ownership of Poona members. The original sketch is shown overleaf.

The Following Years

Nine Tiffins were held in 1935 in a variety of venues, with Reggie again being the most regular attendee.

The weekend of 2nd and 3rd March saw a Tiffin in Oxford on the Saturday with ten attendees, which, since there were fourteen members at the time, was deemed to be a record – 71% attendance. This achievement prompted another Tiffin to be celebrated the following day, which was also the first recorded visit by the Club to two hostelries it would come to know well – firstly The Perch at Binsey, and then onto The Trout at Godstow.

The first overseas Tiffin (and the Club's twenty first) was also held in this year (1935), when Reggie Bennett, Archie Hope, Colin Ratsey and his wife went to America to compete in the Frostbite Gold Cup in Larchmont. While not strictly quorate, with only three members present, it was still deemed a Tiffin and resulted in the Club's first publicity in America:

*The voyage to America of the Commodore and Chaplain proved itself
such a hurrah-party for Poona that the Hon. Sails Manager and*

manageress must be considered, with them, to have formed a quorum. The New York Herald Tribune (Bill Taylor) wrote about the Club and its racing flag. And the joke went down quite absurdly well. Walter Rowe supplied us with topees and we elected him our Mother Superior (honorary).

There was quite a break after this encounter, which was partly caused by the run up to the Olympics in 1936. Colin Ratsey and Reggie Bennett were runners-up in the trials for the Star Class and selected as reserves.

The original drawing of the Cap Badge by Gillie Potter

The Denouement

Only six Tiffins were held in 1936 and none in 1937. It seems that Reggie's time was now filled with other things.

In February 1937, he passed his medical qualifications, and was soon working as a locum around the country. He also contested the London County Council elections in East Woolwich, joined the Royal Naval Volunteer Reserve (RNVR), and was a special constable in the Metropolitan River Police at Wapping, as well as sailing and flying as often as he could.

He spent the following winter in India as pilot to the Maharajah of Rajpipla, and spoke warmly of his time there.

On his return, in 1938, he realised that the Imperial Poona Yacht Club was no longer quorate, as he explained in his memoir:

It [the Imperial Poona Yacht Club] *had a rule which established a quorum* [four] *for any meeting, and another condition was that bachelordom was obligatory. So, as the undergraduates of yesteryear fell away into the arms of matrimony, our numbers had fallen rapidly until just before the war broke out our club had to be dissolved. It was dissolved in the Resident Clerk's room, or Resident Secretary's room, in the Foreign Office, where Charlie Johnston, the Vice Commodore, was then serving. The three remaining bachelors and the fourth, the last backslider, had solemnly toasted the Club and called it off.*

Present on this auspicious occasion, the Club's twenty eigth Tiffin, was Charlie Johnston (Great White Vice), Reggie Bennett (Chaplain), Richard Fairey and Tim Bennett (Reggie's brother).

The Minute Book records the Club being formally dissolved "*as its purpose had been achieved.*"

And so, a Club started on the banks of the Thames was dissolved at the Foreign Office after a brief existence of what appears to have been two active and two inactive years.

The historical notes in the Club's handbook record: "*war followed, though not immediately*".

THE SECOND INCARNATION

The Reformation

The Second World War saw three Poona members lose their lives: Tim Bennett, Philip Wheeler and Arthur Whitehead, and, according to the Minute Book *"the original membership was otherwise altogether scattered."* The record continues:

In 1946, when peace had broken out again, strong hints were given, from both Burnham and Cowes, that the Culture of Poona was once more sadly needed in the world.

The Club was therefore re-formed by five of the original members – Reggie Bennett, Peter Norton, Constable Roberts, Tiny Mitchell and Frank Spriggs – together with eight newly co-opted members, making thirteen members in all.

  The first official Tiffin of the new era was at Hamble on Sunday 28th July 1946 during a match against the Centreboard Racing Club, which Poona won. Cowes Week followed shortly afterwards and all the members bar one (who had been deported to the British Embassy in Brazil) attended.

  Democracy, of a sort, arrived at Poona in the winter of 1946, when the thirteen members were invited to propose candidates for the two vacancies and vote for the Flag Officers. Reggie Bennett was duly elected as Commodore, with Sir Heneage Ogilvie as Great White Vice and Steve Longsdon as Great Gorgeous Rear, although the latter's election was only possible because the rule of disqualification from membership for visiting Poona was waived!

  Coupled with this election, the original Great White Vice, Charles Johnston, returned from diplomatic missions in Japan and Egypt and re-joined the Club, and John Carew-Jones was also elected – filling the fifteen places available.

  As a joke, the Club applied for recognition by the YRA (predecessor to the current RYA) and were rather surprised that some took them more seriously than they took themselves. The Club's name duly appeared both on the list of YRA recognised clubs and the Lloyd's list.

The Redefinition

Six sahibs and six memsahibs (including a Miss Henrietta Crane, making her first appearance in our history) gathered in the Royal Thames Yacht

Club in Knightsbridge on Thursday 19th December 1946 to review the Rules and Constitution and made the following changes:

- The bachelordom rule was removed.
- The disqualification of anyone visiting Poona was amended to require that *"any officer or member who completes a pilgrimage to Poona assumes the style and title of 'hadji' and shall dye his beard blue."*
- The flag of the club was changed to the now customary yellow with three red balls.

Following its own recognition by the YRA, the Club decided to reverse its earlier policy and formally recognised the Yacht Racing Association. This process has continued as it has subsequently recognised the Yachting Association and then the Royal Yachting Association. The Club is committed to a policy of continuing this process as required.

For the first time, an annual subscription of one guinea was imposed, but members who were shocked by such a financial imposition were left in a difficult position: *"Members who feel unable or unwilling to contribute are requested to send in their resignations to the Secretariat Wallah. These resignations will be refused and a fine of two guineas imposed forthwith"*!

However, despite much chasing, three members had failed to pay their subscription some two years later, and they were therefore deemed to have resigned.

But it was not just the members who were having difficulties with the idea of the Club having money. Lloyds Bank were unhappy with the idea of an account being held by a Club in which all its members constituted the committee. To pacify them, a smaller committee had to be established as far as the bank was concerned.

The full membership limit of fifteen was somewhat being ignored at this time, with at least four new members being elected in late 1946 and two old members (Richard Webster and John Palmer) re-joining. At a Tiffin at the Royal Thames Yacht Club in February 1947, the membership was formally increased from fifteen to twenty five, where it remains to this day.

The twenty fifth member was elected a few months later, and a waiting list was established. In order to reduce this, it was decided that any member who had been out of the United Kingdom for twelve consecutive months would be treated as deported and taken off the active list to allow some on the waiting list into membership.

As this waiting list grew, more stringent measures were required, and in 1949 a rule was added that cessation of membership could happen *"temporarily, on imprisonment (whether civil, service or domestic) and deportation.*" As a result, two members ceased to be on the active list for reasons of deportation, two for service imprisonment and one for domestic imprisonment.

Later that year it was also decided that membership would also cease on "*ceasing to think Imperially.*"

On New Year's Day 1950, the active list of members numbered twenty four. In addition there were two on the Deported list, two Honorary members and nine on the waiting list, although it would appear that only one of these ever made it to Active membership.

Tiffins

The Club certainly had a new lease of life, with four Tiffins recorded in the first two months of 1947, and many more throughout the year.

One (with the required four members present) was even held during the Oxford & Cambridge Sailing Society's match against the Dragon Class (Solent Division), indicating that membership of both clubs was no longer frowned upon.

Other Tiffins in 1947 took place on the Clyde and at Cowes and Burnham as members got to grips with the first real season's sailing since the war.

Perhaps the largest gathering of members took place on 27th November 1947, when twelve members and five guests gathered in the Cock Tavern in Fleet Street to mark the last bachelor night of the Commodore and Chaplain, Reggie Bennett.

This was followed, the next day, by the Club's first Durbar – to celebrate the marriage of Reggie and Henrietta. It is recorded: "*This was an orderly affair, whether it was due to the occasion or whether from the night before, it is hard to say.*"

At the next Tiffin a tighter definition of the Club's gatherings was agreed:

- Chota Hazri – up to six members
- Tiffin – seven members and over
- Durbar – full membership

Occasionally Tiffins were made more public, as in February 1949 when a journalist from the Evening Standard "*accidentally attended*" part of one and wrote about it in the 'In London Last Night' section of the paper.

Another large gathering of the Club occurred when fifteen active and two honorary members were present at the Island Sailing Club's Jubilee Dinner and Dance celebrating that Club's 60th anniversary at the Dorchester Hotel in March 1949.

Reggie Bennett's Stag Night, 27th November, 1947

	John Palmer	Jack Dewsberry	Cecil Knight	James Tilney
Joe Brunton	Ernest Harston	Bruce Kinnier-Wilson	Jack Longsdon	Steve Longsdon
				Reggie Bennett
	John Dunn	Tony Tollemache	John Mead	Frank Spriggs
				Peter Norton
	Slim Behenna	Jack Raymond	Mike Crean	

A landmark Chota Hazri (with five members present) took place in January 1950 for the first and only unholy alliance in marriage between two Poona offspring when Douglas Howden Hume (son of James Howden Hume, Honorary Pipah) married June Spriggs (daughter of Sir Frank Spencer Spriggs, Kitehawk).

Tiffins continued apace in 1950 with eight recorded at various sailing clubs and other hostelries around the country.

Sailing

Matches against other clubs were revived in 1949, with a win against Lee-on-Solent SC and losses recorded against the Oxford University YC and Hamble River SC. The latter match attracted quite a bit of press attention because Reggie Bennett was standing for parliament as the Conservative candidate for Gosport and Fareham.

It is interesting to think that in 1949, tales of the Imperial Poona Yacht Club, and its irreverent ways, were felt to be a positive story for a prospective parliamentary candidate and press releases were issued – I suspect the same would not be true in today's "politically correct" environment!

Nevertheless, the match was reported in the Evening Standard, Southern Daily Echo, Hampshire Telegraph & Post and one other unidentifiable newspaper.

Reggie was duly elected with a "*vast majority*" in 1950. One of his first steps was to help create the House of Commons Yacht Club, of which he was appointed as Secretary. The Minute Book records: "*A number of messages were received congratulating him on his first step towards high parliamentary office.*"

The House of Commons YC made its first appearance in public in a three cornered match between themselves, Lee-on-Solent SC and the Imperial Poona YC at Lee-on-Solent on 23rd July 1950. Unfortunately an onshore gale was blowing and the boats could not be launched, so sailing was cancelled. Instead "*a programme of sporting contests*" was organised by Charles Taylor, MP for Eastbourne.

As part of this, a beer drinking race was run, with a team, largely composed of House of Commons YC members, beating a Poona / Lee-on-Solent team. The event was photographed and witnessed by Sir Charles MacAndrew, Deputy Speaker of the House of Commons (and Commodore of the House of Commons YC). Again, something that might not happen (or certainly not be publicly photographed) today, but recorded here to show that politicians did not always take themselves as seriously as they do now.

An attempt to hold this fixture was repeated on 24th September 1950, but this was again unsuccessful.

The match was finally held in the summer of 1951 and reported, with photographs in an unidentified publication, but possibly Country Life. Lee-on-Solent won, Poona was second and the House of Commons bought up the rear.

Poona and the House of Commons YC competed in another three way match, this time against the United Hospitals SC at Burnham on

Crouch in 1951. This again resulted in victory for the home team, with Poona second and the House of Commons third.

Beer Drinking Race Involving The House of Commons YC, Imperial Poona YC and Lee-on-Solent SC, 23rd July, 1950

Winning Team (front to back)
Tufton Beamish, HoCYC
Michael Crean, IPYC
Stephens, HoCYC
Terry Clarke, HoCYC
Charles Taylor, HoCYC
Reggie Bennett, HoCYC, IPYC

Losing Team (front to back)
Joe Hannen, LoSSC, IPYC
Eric Hannen, LoSSC
Gerald Hume Wright, LoSSC
V J van der Byl, LoSSC
James Talbot, IPYC
Hugh Somerville, IPYC
John Chamier, IPYC

The 58th Tiffin

Reggie's election to the House of Commons also provided the opportunity for the Club which mocked the establishment to meet at the heart of it when the 58th Tiffin was held at the House of Commons on Monday 6th November 1950.

It was a working dinner for Reggie as proceedings were interrupted when *"the Commodore withdrew to record his vote at his place of work"*!

Items on the agenda included:

- Defacing our Ensign – rejected on the grounds that it was *"either below or above the Club's dignity."*
- The need for a Sacred Cow – inconclusive.
- A suggestion that one Tiffin a year be for men only – agreed, but changed to *"members only"*.
- Registering disgust that the health of the King Emperor is no longer drunk in the Indian Army – withdrawn on the basis that *"it was virtually impossible to drink anyone's health in India owing to the prohibition."*

The Evening Standard announced the event, but it was an unnamed Irish paper which went to town about it:

Egad, Sir! These Imperial Pooners Take Some Beating

In the British House of Commons last Monday, there was a smashing "do". Twenty-five pukka-pukka sahibs sat down together to have what we might call dinner, but which they elect to call Tiffin. They were members of the Imperial Poona Yacht Club – probably one of the most outrageous sports bodies in the world.

There are sports bodies which are snobbish ... there are bodies which are very snobbish ... but Imperial Poona Yacht Club takes the biscuit. No doubt they have the usual qualifications for an exclusive club, but they have one in addition which we can appreciate fully here and fairly beats Banagher.

They lay down that any man who knows one word of Hindustani (language spoken in Poona) is not eligible for membership, and if, as a member, he learns one word, he has his gold braid and buttons cut off and is drummed out.

I don't believe that, even in its palmist days, the Kildare Street Club would have gone as far as that, even though their views of the Irish language may have been severe.

One can easily imagine the "Imperial Pooners" going about their business with corks in their ears lest they hear words of Hindustani. No doubt they have a Vigilance Committee with their ears cocked waiting for that one word which would mean expulsion. Incidentally, they limit their membership to 25 – but I doubt if there is any need for a limit with such a regulation.

OVERSEAS EXPANSION

By the early 1950s, Poona was firmly re-established in the UK, with regular Tiffins, Chota Hazris and sailing matches. Once the home of the UK government had been invaded in November 1950, thought turned to extending Poona's empire.

Revolting Colonies

In December 1950, there was a meeting specifically called to discuss a crisis over ties – the number ordered from the manufacturer greatly exceeded the number bought by members, and the manufacturer was chasing payment.

At the meeting: *"The Commodore produced photographic evidence that our American Honorary Members were 'thinking Imperially' and it was decided to try to unload the surplus tie stock upon them at a suitably inflated price."*

How these small things shape the course of history. A concern over tea saw the Americans begin to separate from the United Kingdom, but now a crisis over ties saw some strengthening of the bond between Imperial Thinkers on both sides of the Atlantic!

When the US Six Metre team, led by Robert Meyer, came to race against the UK in 1951 there was a meeting with *"the members of the Imperial Poona YC 'Lodge' in the Revolting Colonies ... much business was done including the sale of 15 ties at exorbitant price and the scrutinising of their charter."*

A few days later *"at a simple, though moving, ceremony in London"* on 26th July, 1951, the charter was duly consecrated and signed by Reggie Bennett and Robert Meyer.

As soon as the Revolting Colonies Outpost had been established, and before they had time to regroup on their native soil, a sailing match was held between them and the home station of the Imperial Poona Yacht Club in Cowes. This was held in centre-board sailing dinghies and the Revolting Colonies won.

Three years earlier, Reggie had spotted an old quart beer mug standing on the floor of a Cowes grocer's shop, catching the tap drippings from a barrel of vinegar. With Mr Biddlecomes's consent, he exchanged it for a jam jar.

He titled this the Thunder Mug and presented it to the victors, who proudly took the mug back to Long Island and had it cleaned, mounted and inscribed. It now became a permanent challenge trophy to be competed for whenever the two arms of the Club got together.

CHARTER OF A WESTERN HEMISPHERE STATION
of the
IMPERIAL POONA YACHT CLUB

NAME
: The REVOLTING COLONIES OUTPOST of the IMPERIAL POONA YACHT CLUB.

STATION
: Revolting Colonies Unlimited and the Island of Yap.

MEMBERS
: Twelve and one half Members, all of whom have read "SUBMERSION IS THE BETTER PART OF VALOR" at the Union Inn, Cowes, Isle of Wightistan, UK, or have pursued same philosophy in Imperial waters for a protracted period, except that whenever a Member re-enters the Station of the IMPERIAL POONA YACHT CLUB a vacancy shall be deemed to exist in the membership of the REVOLTING COLONIES OUTPOST Station which may be filled provided that the total membership never exceeds twenty-five Members. No memsahibs are eligible.

SUB-MOTTO
: "LET US BE REVOLTING" to be executed in Latin and Indian by the Revolting Charge of Intimate Imperial Home Relations.

OFFICERS
: The Officers of the Station shall consist of: The RCO Commodore, the RCO Great White Vice, the RCC Great Gorgeous Rear, the RCO Secretariat-Wallah, the RCO Finance Member, an Honorary Chaplain, the Secretariat-Wallah of the Recently-Impressed Late-Deported, the Revolting Charge of Intimate Imperial Home Relations, the RCO Serang, the RCO Djinn-Krooboy, The RCO Donkeyman, the RCO Punkah-Wallah, the RCO Shanty-Muezzin, the RCO Currie-Fellah, and any others that may hereafter be instituted.

TIFFIN
: A bi-annual Tiffin shall be held whenever circumstances require during the Monsoon season, and a bi-annual Tiffin shall be held whenever circumstances require during the Dry season, and at Tiffin the toast of "Poona" shall always be drunk and shall always be followed by the toast of "Let us be revolting."

ET ALIA
: The Rules and Constitution of the Imperial Poona Yacht Club shall govern in cases of doubt.

AUTHORITY
: LETTER DATED 26 July 1951 from Commodore Dr. Reginald Bennett, VRD, MP.

After The Signing Of The Revolting Colonies Charter, 26th July, 1951

Back row: Jack Maclay, Trevor de Hamel, Buddy Bombard, Sir Heneage Ogilvie, Alan Priddy, Wilson Cross, Stan Priddy, John Morgan, John Palmer, Glen Foster, Peter Macdonald
Front row: Charles Taylor, Magnus Konow, Charlie MacAndrew, Robert Meyer Jr., Osborne Dobell, Reggie Bennett, Robert Meyer Sr.

A newspaper report of this first match between the two teams concludes:

In the contest there is but one rule governing the competition craft. It is that the competition is limited to sailboats 'having no more than one design each', a joke which will appeal to racing yachtsmen.

The Imperial Poona Yacht Club was born among undergraduates at Oxford in 1931 [actually 1934]. *Dr Bennett was among those who started it as a satirical, but good humoured, comment on the social importance attached, by some military men of those days, to service in Poona. The reason for it has gone, but the spirit and comradeship have survived.*

After all this activity in 1951, 1952 appears to have been a quiet year, with just one event recorded – the annual match against the Oxford University

YC. Those who know how this match developed in later years may be surprised to know that the racing was conventional, with no strange rules.

The rules used later actually originated in North America when, during the Autumn of 1953, Reggie Bennett and other Poona members were there for the races against America in the Six metre class. Once again, the original Imperial Poona Yacht Club competed against the Revolting Colonies for the Thunder Mug.

This was reported in the Times, on 30th September, by a 'special correspondent' – special in that he was the IPYC's Commode, Reggie Bennett. The report is reprinted here by kind permission of Times Newspapers.

THE THUNDER MUG

BRITISH YACHTSMEN BRING IT HOME
FROM OUR SPECIAL CORRESPONDENT
OYSTER BAY, SEPT. 28

Yesterday morning, after a month's season of international racing in the six-metre class, a team race in centre board boats was organized. This was for the Thunder Mug, that battered old pewter quart pot that once did menial service in Cowes and now stands engraved on a plinth here – though not for long.

The class sailed for the purpose was the Ravens. These are large, powerful, half-deckers, 24ft. long, carrying a 200lb. centreplate. Ravens are exceedingly fast – they usually catch up six-metres – and they plane readily up to 12-15 knots. Their owners and crews are understandably enthusiastic and, to other less active yachtsmen, are generally known as "Raven maniacs". The winner and runner-up of the national Raven championships in Ohio earlier this month, J. Roosevelt's Old Crow and H. Anderson's Sleipnir, were in yesterday's event and the racing was keen.

The course was from the club pontoon, about half a mile to windward, through the anchorage, to the great schooner Guinevere, twice round this ship in either direction, then a reach to a small seaplane moored near the beach off Centre Island, then back to the club pontoon, the finishing line to be crossed stern first. A nice south-west breeze was blowing.

Soon after the third gun the race officer, D. Jewett, announced the start, and the boats feverishly cast off and pushed one another off. In the melee J. Harrison was left, but made a very fast tack along the face of the pontoon while the rest were making their way through the anchored six-metre class. The rule that port tack had right of way produced many interesting situations, as did the various encounters while rounding

28

Guinevere. E. Ridder, in Gizmo, did great things in assisting his colleagues, and the seaplane turning-point was passed without any disqualifications. Of course, the final sternboard through the line was most spectacular. Gizmo assisting the commodore's boat astern to such good effect that the race was awarded on corrected times to the Imperial Poona Yacht Club, protests received, and copiously attested, not having been upheld.

The Thunder Mug thus returns to Great Britain, the only trophy to do so during the great sailing season here that is now drawing to a close. It is good that we do not return empty-handed, and we can assure our American hosts that we shall go back with our hearts full of their kindness and sportsmanship, awaiting eagerly our chance to entertain them in our waters in 1955.

Repulsive, But Not Revolting, Colonies

On 22nd April 1955, exactly twenty one years after the Imperial Poona Yacht Club was founded, the Club established its second overseas outpost – the Repulsive But Non-Revolting Canadian Outpost at Toronto.

The Repulsive, But Not Revolting, Colonists During A Sail Past In 1962

However, this international expansion caused problems with the monetary basis of the Club. Bill Gooderham, the Repulsive Commodore wrote:

Regarding annual fees and entrance fees: the Constitution is set up for payment in rupees; as they are very scarce in the locality of our outpost could we use some other type of wampum [the North American Indian currency], *that being anything which might be barter-able . We would suggest an ounce of uranium, rum, or something else that is easier to obtain than rupees.*

The Reactionary Colonies

The third Poona outpost was in Bermuda and called the Reactionary Colonies. The Club's handbook states that this was "*duly founded on a date now lost in the mists of history*", and the first documentary evidence of it is from the mid 1960s, but it was clearly up and running before then, although not before 1957.

The outpost's own charter and constitution (dated 1986) is no more informative, stating:

Whereas, on a date which is lost to the memory of man, but generally taken to be the 22nd day of April in One Thousand Nine Hundred and something (being the anniversary of the date on which The Great Philanthropic and Benevolent Institution known as the Imperial Poona Yacht Club was founded) a group of like-minded and Imperially-thinking Pukka Sahibs caused a Bermuda Outpost of the said Imperial Poona Yacht Club to be established in Hamilton in the Colony of Bermuda known as the "Reactionary Colonists' Outpost" or the "Reactionary Onions".

They too revolted against the traditional currency of the rupee, and, instead, used Bermuda Pearl Onions (Gin soaked).

As well as having backwards races like that held in America in 1953, the Bermuda outpost introduced the backwards Tiffin, starting with the cigars and brandy and working their way towards the soup.

DEVELOPMENTS AT HOME

Meanwhile the 1950s saw the British home station of the Imperial Poona Yacht Club flourish, and an influx of new blood.

The Club maintained its limit of twenty five active members, with candidates mostly, but not exclusively, proposed by Reggie Bennett and then submitted to the membership for approval. Generally prospective members were good sailors who shared Reggie's sense of fun, a number being graduates from the Oxford University Yacht Club, although this was certainly not the only source of members.

Uffa Fox

Reggie first met Uffa Fox (the renowned boat designer, sailor and character) in 1929 when he sailed his dinghy across to the Isle of Wight while still at Winchester College. He happened to walk past someone working on an upturned 14 ft dinghy and asked him where he could get fresh water and whether he knew a person called Uffa Fox who lived round there. It was Uffa himself, working on the celebrated 'Avenger'. This started a lifelong association between the two characters which Reggie recalls was *"attended by many a remarkable event, always amusing."*

One such event was when Uffa revived the playing of cricket on the Brambles sand bank in the Solent on 15th September 1954. Uffa captained a Yachtsmen of Cowes team against Parkhurst Prison. As the tide went out, Reggie and Mike Parker planted the Imperial Poona burgee in the sand and the game proceeded until the sands began to be covered again. Near the end, the Governor of Parkhurst Prison vanished under water suddenly when running backwards for a high catch. The Times reported the match saying *"no doubt the venue was chosen with a view to preventing the escape of any of the players"*!

Uffa was elected to the Club in 1955 and Time Magazine also recorded the presence of both Uffa and the Imperial Poona Yacht Club at Cowes Week in that year in an article entitled *'Renaissance Man'*. This article talked about Uffa donning a pith helmet and leading the Imperial Poona Yacht Club in song. The article can be found by typing "Imperial Poona Yacht Club" into Google, but sadly the rights to reproduce even a paragraph of it here were prohibitively expensive.

Cricket On The Brambles, 15ᵗʰ September, 1954
The Yachtsmen Of Cowes Against Parkhurst Prison

Backward Races

While we have reported on matches against Oxford, these had taken the form of conventional team races, but, following the innovations seen in the race for the Thunder Mug in America in 1953, the rules changed somewhat.

In 1955, a rule was introduced into the IPYC constitution that *"An annual race shall be held from time to time in the cradle of the Backward Races."* The cradle of the Backward Races is, of course, Oxford and there were three simple rules for these races:

1. On the windward leg, port tack has right of way.
2. On reaching a mark, the mark has got to be hit. Rounding it without hitting it is not valid.
3. The downwind leg must be sailed backwards.

These reverse the standard rules of sailing where starboard tack has right of way, and marks must be rounded, but not touched. There is nothing in the usual rules to say which direction any leg has to be sailed, but backwards is certainly not the conventional, fastest or easiest approach. However, with practise, it is not only possible to sail effectively downwind backwards, but also to get a dinghy to plane in this manner!

The races traditionally took place in early November, partly to tie in with the celebrations at this time associated with the *"only person who has entered Parliament honestly"* (as MP Reggie described him), but it had the added advantage that it coincided with the International Yacht Racing Union's annual meetings which were held in London. This enabled some members of the Club's Outposts, who were in England for the meetings, to attend.

The best account of the match is provided by the then Secretariat-Wallah (later Commode) of the Revolting Colonies Outpost, Harry Anderson, reporting back to his members on the strange happenings on the banks of the Thames. Harry Anderson attended several of these matches over the years, even once when he was Chairman of the New York Yacht Club's America's Cup Committee which was facing a challenge from the UK. He described the 1965 match in the form of a play, and has kindly given permission for this to be reproduced here. (This was also featured in the American Sailor magazine in their April 1992 edition, which was a special "Fun Racing Issue". They added two cartoons by Scott Getchell which are reproduced here with the kind permission of the US Sailing Association).

ACT I

Scene 1.   *Main room and bar of the pub 'The Perch' set back from the west bank of the Thames upstream from the Medley weir.*

In rain which is characterized locally as 'a bit of a spill' we skirt the sentinel – a boxer as uncommunicative as he is unflinching – and enter the pub to be greeted by Commodore Bennett decked in houndstooth.

The enthusiasm with which the members of the Home Station and their memsahibs and sub-memsahibs greet the R.C.O. [Revolting Colonies Outpost] envoy is reciprocated and quickly leads to thirst-slaking.

The Perch, already bulging with a medley of Poona members from the Active List and graduate and undergraduate members of the Oxford University Yacht Club so that the majority are perforce on their feet with heads bowed in the act either of quaffing another draught of bitters or of avoiding contact with one of the central ceiling rafters, is soon reinforced by those 'regulars' who dare brave the assemblage and by occasional fishermen seeking refuge from the weather.

It should be interposed that the 'Home Station' of the Poona, even more so than that of the R.C.O., takes an active interest in yachting among the University Clubs and enjoys a long tradition of replenishing its ranks from among graduates of the Oxford University Yacht Club. Oxford being the 'Cradle of The Backward Races', the annual regatta is quite appropriately conducted under their auspices.

Scene 2:   Dining room & side bar of the pub 'The Perch'.
Time: Wine and luncheon.
Although almost forty strong, twice the number for which arrangements
have been made, Proprietor Chitty jovially and resourcefully meets the
exigencies in the best tradition, and all hands, having attained a state of
well-being in inverse ratio to the conditions prevailing outside, commence
devouring a succulent deep-dish pie washed down with the finest Rhenish.
Most colourful are the vestments ranging from the IPYC Commodore's

34

Sherlock Holmes ensemble, the Oxford UYC Vice Commodore's red and white striped shirt and every variety of the International Finn Class President, Vernon Stratton's, self-rescuing jackets worn by those who decline to rely on tweeds-against-the-Thames.

Scene 3:   *Same as Scene 2*
Time: *Port after luncheon.*
As luncheon pales, the port is poured, but inasmuch as a matter of serious business is raised from the floor, so a concomitant hue and cry is raised for more port to sustain the proceedings. Proprietor Chitty thereupon ransacks for sack and Commodore Bennett calls for a semblance of order. Same is gradually achieved, and the matter is put before the house regarding the sad state of morality among the members of the R.C.O. resulting in the resignation in the preceding decade of Honorary Chaplain, Commander C. Sherman Hoyt, under Rule 9 (a) [the rule requiring membership to cease on death]. *The four I.P.Y.C. members present who had completed pilgrimages to the shores of Oyster Bay in the R.C.O. home territory cite the uplifting effect which they experienced under the exhilarating influence of R.C.O. member 'Have-A-Scoop', Morgan S.A. Reichner, at which point in the proceedings, there being none contrary minded, there arises such a deafening clamor of approbation (we note that coincidentally the Proprietor is espied arriving with the afore-mentioned reinforcements of sack so it is not too clear whether developments serious or savory spark the clamor) that the Commodore hastens to declare his appointment as R.C.O. Chaplain duly confirmed.*

At this juncture one member of the gathering unwittingly unlatches a window against which another member is propped (space is somewhat at a premium today in The Perch, hence this precarious one), and the latter is bouleversed to the terrace. On recovering his aplomb he declares a slight diminution in the prevailing effluvium, and all hands proceed forthwith to the river bank.

ACT II

Scene 1:   *On the west bank of the southwest elbow of the Thames above the bend above the Medley Weir Bridge. A sparse scattering of trees and bushes line the bank and extend inland bifurcating the grasslands tangentially to the bank. At a small dock, nine Alphas (akin to Fireflies but built of fibreglass) are secured.*
The Race Officer takes his station under an umbrella with whistle and a quiver of two dozen rockets – the starting signal being the eleventh rocket to flare. It is never quite clear what point on the east bank constitutes the

other end of the line, although as the contest evolves the question becomes more and more academic. Distributed up and downstream along the west bank are single fishermen seated beneath black or green umbrellas (the choice of colour presumably depending on their personal piscatorial predilections), but by mid-afternoon all gradually beat a retreat to escape from the inclement weather.

The east bank comprises a vast meadow (whence the appellation 'Port Meadow') stretching to the outskirts of Oxford whose spires and towers are visible in the distance. Stray cows graze the meadow and at the edge of the bank several score of geese are crouched ready to slip into the river and surround an unsuspecting Alpha.

I.P.Y.C. members, perhaps because of their advanced stage of edification, are not scheduled to participate on the first few races. The system of rocket starts seems to be working reasonably well, umbrellas work only with partial success and the underfooting is gradually deteriorating. It becomes increasingly difficult to sort out the O.U.Y.C. fleet from the fleet of the Medley Sailing Club whose downstream mark is farther downstream than, and whose upstream mark is farther upstream than, the respective rounding marks of the O.U.Y.C.

Scene 2:   *Same place*
Time: *Late afternoon*
At a suitable interval before dusk Poona enters the lists and the Secretariat-Wallah of the R.C.O. in towncoat and Homburg takes the helm with Yeti, Brian Appleton, as fore-deck man and connoisseur. Port tack has right of way which, since all yachts have to sail the leeward legs going backwards, contributes towards clearing up any possible confusion in the minds of the helmsmen of the Medley Sailing Club yachts, inasmuch as a port tack yacht sailing backwards is, for the purpose of another yacht sailing forward, ipso facto on the starboard tack close-hauled (since with the mainboom being held into the wind two-blocked to the shrouds there is no way to sail any closer to the wind with main filled).

After thirteen rockets a re-assemblage, or general recall of sorts, relegates the R.C.O. entry from the vanguard to the ruck. However, a third crew member in the form of Brian Appleton's fiancée, Susan, is plucked from the bank. Thus reinforced, the R.C.O. entry manoeuvres through a maze of what could best be described as the shambles of the once proud fleets of Poona and Oxford. R.C.O. is first yacht to 'bump' (rounding the marks being a method of yacht racing fit only for infidels and serving to create insoluble problems under the archaic, Beowulfian body of lore colloquially referred to in London as the 'I.Y.R.U. Racing Rules') the weather mark and to commence the retrograde movement upstream sailing backwards. Sowar ke Batcha, Noel Dobbs, is observed abandoning a sinking Alpha and swimming to shore, one arm aloft in an attempt to keep his timepiece dry – almost as futile a gesture under the circumstances as attempting to keep his codpiece dry. Simultaneously three Alphas become engaged in such a manner that all three capsize, the mast and rig of the weather yacht emerging clear and to leeward of the leeward-most yacht – clearly an instance of the weather yacht luffing two yachts overlapped to leeward and cause, therefore, only for 'Imperial' censure under the doctrine 'de minimis non curat lex'.

Several of the crew members take to the river and proceed to attempt to right the above-mentioned sunken yacht which is now bow deep in the mud (it being the practice of backward races to use the bow tank covers to entrap the halyard tails, thereby creating an aperture and violating their watertight integrity). The stern tank, however, remains dry which, considering the fact that the transom is pointed majestically skyward, demonstrates that the Alpha is almost as aerodynamically sound in still flight as the Poona Swettipore One Designs.

By now the melange of Alphas capsized, Medley Sailing Club craft circumnavigating the same, O.U.Y.C. Vice Commodore Tony Lunch porposing about amidst the cackle of geese (having followed the sage advice of WW1 submarine motto over the bar at the Union Inn at Cowes to the effect that 'Submersion is the better part of Valor') are becoming indistinguishable in the miasma of deepening dusk prompting the R.C. Officer to empty his quiver of the final cluster of rockets and call a halt to the proceedings.

Scene 3:   Denouement – downstream above the Medley Weir
                Bridge
The flotilla limps upwind, downstream, recovering the R.C.O.'s Homburg which is floating ahead and all yachts are beached for the night.

ACT III
Scene 1:   In Oxford proper at the headquarters of the Oxford
                University Yacht Club – Committee Room.
Time: Low Tea.
By various conveyances and stages, contestants and spectators assemble at the honorary and ancient headquarters of the O.U.Y.C. and partake of tea, switch to dry vestments and await the summations of the score-keepers. At this juncture the final business of the meeting is transacted, namely that it be the mission of the I.P.Y.C. to construct a scoring system for use in the Olympic Yachting Games that will be a test of the competitors the equivalent of the test of that competition. It is also the consensus that the R.C.O. Secretariat-Wallah, being an ex-Rear-Commodore of the Yale Yacht Club, will ship a burgee of said Club for display alongside the collection to be seen in the next scene.

Scene 2:   Same hostelry – draught and dart room.
Time: High Tea.
As a result of a certain diurnal process, ascribable to the local statutes, the assemblage migrates across the hallway to engage in quaffing and a

match of darts between Oxford and Poona teams each supplemented by memsahibs and sub-memsahibs. The match threatens to last almost as long as the recent regatta so a second keg of bitters is tapped when suddenly it comes to a resounding conclusion in favour of the I.P.Y.C. when on the 12th round of play R.C.O. Secretariat-Wallah pierces the 'bull' with his second throw of the round – it should be noted that he had meticulously declined to play the red-feathered set, preferring those tipped in Yale blue.

Scene 3:   *No change in scene.*
Time: *Considerable change in time.*
At this juncture all are feeling imperially to such a degree that it is the thinking, even among the backward races, that, since it is no longer possible to distinguish by their actions, graduate from undergraduate, or friend from foe, it is time to lower the curtain and thus conclude a most memorable occasion.

Too long constrain'd by civilization's traces,
Let's seek surcease amongs't the Backwards Races.

Perhaps unsurprisingly, this event has attracted some press coverage over the years, with varying degrees of amusement and understanding. The Tatler despatched a journalist and photographer for an article which appeared in the 15th November 1961 edition.

This was a sympathetic account which included the following:

Imperial Poona has an active list of about 25 headed by Prince Philip [to be explained in the next chapter]. *All of them are men who have made a name for themselves in competitive sailing and all of them have a passionate belief that sailing should be fun.... Boys of all ages who have fallen in love with boats assembled at the Perch, either to sail or to watch. There were the Poona people broad-shouldered with strong-boned faces and a couple of authoritatively greying hairs. The Oxford men were tall, wonderfully fit looking, and they all seemed to have those alert, restless eyes that don't easily let opportunity slip.... Dr Bennett was quickly in the lead. But a rowdy-looking Oxford boat came up and with remarkable fleetness and dexterity pinched the rudder! .....As the afternoon wore on the sheer indestructibility of English yachtsmen was manifestly apparent. Mr David Prior-Palmer, son of Sir Otho and a noted Christ Church skier and debater, was in a challenging position in an Oxford boat when he sat on a firework which propelled him into the river.*

The article even has photographic evidence of this last incident!

The Poona Team for the 1961 Backwards Races At Oxford

Back row: Brian Appleton, Mike Ford, Jamie Dobbs
Middle row: John Chamier, Noel Dobbs, Steven Longsdon, Peter Hunter, Hugh Somerville
Front row (prostrate): Reggie Bennett

A less sympathetic article appeared many years later in an Oxford newspaper when the author of this history was an undergraduate and organising the match. A friend, who wrote for this newspaper, wrote a fair account of the match, but his editor chose to modify it. The original piece was top and tailed with the following paragraphs:

Opening Paragraph
Oxford's reputation as a mecca for boorish aristocracy was confirmed on Sunday when members of the Imperial Poona Yacht Club caused heads to turn at The Perch public house in Binsey.

Closing Paragraph
Meanwhile, Oxford's jobless and homeless continue to increase.

It only remains for me to tail this account with the observation that the afore-mentioned editor was later required to spend time at the Her Majesty, the Queen Empress's, pleasure, which cannot, to my knowledge, be said of any member of the Imperial Poona Yacht Club!

The Backwards races took place in the 1950s and 60s, but the undergraduates lost interest for a period in the mid 1970s. They were revived in 1979 by Tony Lunch (who featured in Harry Anderson's play as an undergraduate) when Commodore of the OUYC. He was promptly elected a Poona member and appropriately called Tiffin. The races continued until the mid 1990s.

Silver Jubilee Dinner

This was held in The Royal Thames Yacht Club on 13th November 1959, with the original Commodore and joint-founder, Sir Archibald Hope, renewing his acquaintance with the Club and attending.

Imperial Poona Yacht Club Silver Jubilee Dinner, 13th November, 1959

Back row: Frank Murdoch, David Colville, Trevor de Hamel, Mike Ford, Sir Frank Spriggs, Brian Appleton, Glynn Blaxter, Jimmy Howden Hume, Charles Blake, Mike Parker
Middle row: Sir Heneage Ogilvie, Capt. Walter Rowe, Sir Archibald Hope, Prince Philip, Reggie Bennett, Rupert Kilkelly, Hugh Somerville, Osborne Dobell, Mike Crean, James Talbot, John Carew-Jones
Front row: Jim Orr, Joe Mellor, Uffa Fox, John Chamier

41

PRINCE PHILIP & HIS POT

A certain Prince Philip may have been noticed in the preceding photograph and his presence needs to be explained.

Reggie Bennett got to know Prince Philip through both being members of the Thursday Club. This was a club which consisted of around thirty scriptwriters, humorists and others, founded by a photographer called Baron, whose circle of friends, including Prince Philip, made up the Club. Reggie recalled that they met "*every Thursday with the ostensible reason of compelling the weekend to begin on Thursday lunchtime*" and that "*wit, of course, ran riot.*"

The story goes that Reggie happened to be wearing a Poona tie (yellow, with red balls) one day, and Prince Philip asked him what club it was for. When Reggie replied that it was "*a load of balls*", Prince Philip replied that he liked that and would like to join.

He was therefore elected an Honorary Member Extraordinary. (Reggie was quoted in the Daily Mail in August 1983 saying of the Imperial Poona Yacht Club: "*There are only 25 members and they all have to be fantastic sailors to qualify – Prince Philip is only an honorary member*").

Being an honorary member did not, of course, prevent a Poona name being given, and he was grandly entitled His Highness The Maharaja of Cooch Parwani.

The Maharaja soon made a few suggestions for changes to the rules of the Club.

It may be recalled that these stated that membership would terminate automatically on "*ceasing to think Imperially*". The Maharaja suggested that a footnote be added to the effect that "*ceasing to think shall not necessarily suspend or terminate membership*".

The rules had also required every member present at a Tiffin to make a speech. John Chamier noted, in an article about the Club in the 1979 Christmas edition of The Field, a consequence of this: "*At one of these splendorous happenings one member of flag rank is noted as making the same speech three times before falling asleep at a fourth attempt.*" (Reproduced with kind permission of The Field).

News of this, and possibly his experience of sitting through too many formal dinners, led the Maharaja to suggest the rule be changed to: "*At Tiffin every member present may be capable of speech.*"

Both these rule changes were felt to be welcome additions to Poona's code and were adopted in 1955.

Two years later the Maharaja made perhaps his most significant contribution to the Club and, indeed, to sailing at Cowes, this being before the Cowes Combined Clubs Committee was formed. Reggie recalls that Prince Philip *"thought that the clubs at Cowes spent more time looking down their noses at one another rather than sailing against each other, so he presented a cup to make them sail against one another. So the five clubs at Cowes, of which Poona of course must be included, raced against each other for years and years."*

Uffa Fox, Tiny Mitchell, Reggie Bennett and David Colville met on 11th August 1957 to flesh out the idea, and Uffa sent the plan to Prince Philip, who was at Balmoral, the next day.

Five clubs were to be invited to participate:

> Royal Yacht Squadron
> Royal London Yacht Club
> Royal Corinthian Yacht Club
> Island Sailing Club
> Imperial Poona Yacht Club

The races were to be held in a selected one-design keelboat *"in the Solent during the Parliamentary recess, clear of Cowes Week."* Each club was to compete with a crew of amateur members of the club they represented.

These suggestions obviously met with royal approval, and the agreement of the clubs concerned, because the 1957 event was held in the International One Design Class under the burgee of the Royal Corinthian Yacht Club on Saturday 24th August and Sunday 25th August 1957.

The winning helmsman was to be awarded the HRH Prince Philip, Duke of Edinburgh's, Challenge Cup and the winning club the Imperial Poona Yacht Club Plaque.

Uffa Fox helmed the Imperial Poona Yacht Club team, with Reggie Bennett, John Chamier and Mike Ford as crew, to victory with three second places. A telegram was immediately despatched to Balmoral stating:

SAHIB'S SUPERIOR SAILING SKILL SECURES PRINCE PHILIP'S POONA POT

The next day Uffa wrote a long account of the event for Prince Philip. His covering letter read:

> *My Dear Prince Philip,*
>
> *This is a very long letter giving a true and faithful report of the first series of races that you have invented for us. I would like you not to attempt to read it until you have half an hour or so to while away and then you can picture us storming round the courses, sometimes in charge of the I.O.D.'s and sometimes the I.O.D.'s taking charge of us.*
>
> *I hope you will enjoy all this and if you only get one hundredth part of fun out of imagining our struggles as we slashed through the seas, it will be well worth my while writing this description.*
>
> *Best wishes,*
>
> > *Yours ever*
> >
> > *Uffa*

With such a billing from Uffa, it is only right to include his full account here.

Saturday 24th August came in with a westerly gale that continued throughout the day, which meant that each of the three races would be full of zest, zip and demand a great deal of skill and seamanship on the part of the helmsmen and crews in order to sail the boats round the course under full sail, and the other four boats in the race would increase the intensity of the struggle.

The first course set was K. All marks to port, Prince Consort, East Bramble, West Bramble, East Gurnard to line.

The boats, the International One Design, a Six Metre type hull with a cabin top, with a lead keel, a large mainsail and a small jib and no runners to work. Fast, sensible and seaworthy boats that could be driven to the utmost and still survive.

There were to be five races in five boats and the complete crew, with helmsmen, to change boats at every race.

I am the helmsman of the Imperial Poona Yacht Club boat with Doctor Reginald Bennett, John Chamier and Michael Ford as crew. The first boat we are in is Two Ton Tiny Mitchell's Boat, "Windflower", No. 10.

The start is a run and so we decide to be the outer boat and reach out across the line, keeping just the right side of it until the gun goes, when we shall square right away and set the spinnaker. We have an ebb tide taking us to the westward and so keeping us the right side of the line, so can be hard up on the line all the way out. One of my crew, at one moment, suggested that I could get a bit closer to the line but I pointed out to him that we were laying down at fifty and sixty degrees, according to the squalls, and he in the centre line of the boat had to take into allowance the fact that our great long mast was a long way to leeward of his eyes, that any part of the boat over the line would cause us to be recalled.

We made the best start and our spinnaker was going up with smoke still showing from the gun. Then Bobbie Lowein, the steersman of the Island Sailing Club's boat, "Margaret", No. 7, started to luff across our stern and if we had to respond to his luff, we should have soon been in great trouble with our spinnaker and so I let him go to windward. The effect of this was that he shielded some of the wind out of our spinnaker while it was being set and so helped, instead of hindering, as was his plan, the setting of our spinnaker.

Away we went at a terrific pace for the East Bramble Buoy, four mile dead to leeward.

The different boats in the fleet set their spinnakers and soon the lot of us were rolling and tearing along through the water, making a vigorous and exciting picture.

About a third of the way to the buoy our spinnaker halyard parted with a bang, but we had this aboard before it could get under water and my crew had actually started to take in the spinnaker, but I said, "Oh no. Up you go Michael and re-reeve the spinnaker halyard." So up Michael went, while Reggie Bennett muzzled the spinnaker on deck. To make Michael's work of climbing the mast a little easier, I luffed as soon as they had drawn up level with us across the stern of the Royal Yacht Squadron's boat, for this did two things. It cut their wind, got them interested in a little luffing match and also laid the boat down to an angle so that the mast was about thirty degrees from the upright, instead of being plumb, so making it easier to climb, and also meant that we were going into less tide, which was against us, and if there was any advantage, we should have the inside turn at the mark when we came upon it.

It was quite a struggle for Michael up the mast, but he finally rove off the spinnaker halyard, but just as he came down below the cross-tree I saw that it was round the jumper stays, so he had to climb back another six feet to reeve it off clear. That was the hardest bit of his climb. Down he came, and making fast the spinnaker halyard, soon had the spinnaker set again and away we ran for the buoy. As we came near the buoy, we were running quite dead, I gybed over on to the starboard tack once the spinnaker had come down and so had the right of way as well as calling for room at the mark, and we rounded the mark in third place, with two boats well ahead of us.

It was quite an exciting mark as we had to gybe and then come right up close hauled and tack immediately we could – all of which was carried out successfully and soon we were standing over to the Island shore and a stronger fair tide on the starboard tack. The two boats ahead soon followed.

45

As we stood on and on across, I eased the jib just a little and the main a bit more, for there was far more than these boats could stand in the steep Solent seas, with this weight of wind. We forged our way through the fleet and went to windward.

Meanwhile, John Chamier, who was on the mainsheet, and myself, looked and looked and looked for the West Bramble Buoy – our next mark, but never did once see it. The result was we overstood by something like quarter of a mile and this dropped us back into second place where we stayed for the hard reach across from the West Bramble, with the west going tide, to the East Gurnard, and then a run from the East Gurnard up over the line with the spinnaker set fairly close in shore to avoid the worst of the tide.

One or two of the boats had sustained damage in their spinnaker gear, and only enthusiasts would have set spinnakers on such a day, and so we decided not to have two races in the morning but two in the afternoon and to get these things put right while we were enjoying our lunch.

Meantime, one of the boats had to be replaced by Jack Harrison's brand-new I.O.D., and as all the rigging was unstretched and the sails quite new, Jack thought that he would like to steer his boat so that, if anyone carried the mast away, it would be him.

So for the second race, the Great Gorgeous Rear, John Chamier, stood down for the Gross Vater Colonel Jack Harrison and I came off the tiller and went on to the mainsheet.

Because of the gale, the Starting Committee wisely decided to send us on a very short and easy course for the middle race so that we could endure and the boats endure for the final race, which would be a hard one.

This second course set, was the reverse of E. Line, to Old Castle Point, Thorn Knoll, East Gurnard and the Line. Again, the start was off the wind but this time it was a broad reach with no spinnakers to be set. We all arrived at Old Castle Point in a heap with the Island Sailing Club's boat just ahead and we the second boat round, and being a reach, we continued in this order round the course until the finish, for it was a close reach across to Thorn Knoll, a reach back to the East Gurnard, and a short run home to the finish.

We had our spinnaker on the bow already to set and the halyard attached by one of the Swedish snap-hooks that when you press a button spring open, but these often have a dreadful knack of springing themselves open. This one did this and as Reggie Bennett hoisted away on the halyard, all he did was to take the halyard aloft and not the sail. So we had to finish and keep our second place without a spinnaker and we managed to do this by getting close up under the rocks and in out of the *tide, so that no-one else could get to weather of us, and being less tide, also take our wind. Once again, the Imperial Poona boat was second, and, once again, the Island Sailing Club's boat was first.*

Now came the final race of the day. By now, it was blowing harder than ever. Reggie Bennett went to the Island Sailing Club's crew and said would they mind Jack Harrison steering his own boat as it was all new and he was afraid of the rigging going, or something carrying away, but they, being very earnest about the race, said "No", and that as Jack had seen the mast stand for one race he thought it was all right for the next and so Bobbie Lowein steered the Island Sailing Club's boat in the third race of the day.

We could almost lay the first mark from the weather end of the line but in here there was little fair tide although we were right up in the weather berth, but for all that I decided to start in there, but through interference with other boats, we started with little or no way on but, even so, in this weight of wind, there was enough wind in-shore to keep us in the weather berth and in the first place.

Meantime, out to leeward in a strong fair tide, Paddy Quennell was driving along at a great speed in Tiny Mitchell's boat and when he tacked he would be on starboard tack with right of way, which is worth always three boats length and on such an exciting day as this, perhaps even more.

Immediately he tacked, although he was a long way away, I also tacked to starboard so that I could tack for the buoy well clear of anyone else, and planned to give myself enough room to go under Paddy Quennell's stern on the starboard tack, slide through his lee and so make the buoy first, he having to give me room at the mark even if I had not got through his lee. There are very few people in this world who can resist crossing another boat on the starboard tack when they have right of way, but here Paddy showed great restraint and judgement for, as we approached him on the port tack, he went about before we arrived, knowing that he could make the mark, and I, diving away to go under his stern, when my crew yelled that he had got into irons, so we luffed up our stem, missing his stern by the thickness of a cigarette paper, and away we went to windward of him and on around the mark ahead.

At the mark, the main sheet could not be eased and I was unable to hold our boat "Arrow", No. 5, out of the wind, and so we reached across for Calshot instead of being able to make our gybe round the buoy and run up for the Prince Consort on the starboard gybe, in out of the worst of the tide.

Meanwhile, Paddy Quinnell had rounded the buoy and, being in a little less tide than us, soon came up abreast and made gybing impossible until he did. Now, instead of sailing at the Prince Consort buoy, we are sailing a course forty-five degrees from it, at the Calshot Lightship.

I pointed out to Paddy that we were miles off course and that we could not gybe until he did, and eventually he gybed and in doing so tore some bits out of "Windflower's" sail and then we gybed without damage, so all was well as far as the first two boats were concerned.

Meantime, the Royal London Yacht Club boat, instead of gybing, had gone about to come through the wind to get on to the other gybe and so dropped further astern.

Bobbie Lowein, sailing Jack Harrison's new boat, failed to get the mainsail off the crosstrees and so, when he gybed, split the mainsail and had to give up. We, of course, were delighted that he was out of the race and thought this was nothing but justice and it meant that we would be in the lead for points.

Meanwhile, Paddy Quennell's boat "The Pirate", sailed by the Royal Yacht Squadron's team, was chasing away before the wind and heading straight for the Brambles. She did a gybe, but only half of the sail went over as the top half was caught on the crosstree, so they gybed back again to clear this and, after sometime, finally decided to put her through the wind instead of gybing and eventually came round and on to the course for the Peel Bank buoy. Here was Paddy, the owner of the boat, close aboard us trying to sail Tiny Mitchell's "Windflower" into first place and, at the same time, wondering, first of all, if his own boat, "Pirate II" would survive the two Chinese gybes and being quite certain in his own mind that, if she did, she would finally finish up a wreck on the Brambles itself. However, all was well, and she finished the course safely without any damage.

Meantime, we were roaring away through Cowes Road, diving our bows under seas, so much so, that our Pilgrim Father, the masthead man wanted to go forward to get the spinnaker off the stemhead, but I pointed out to him that once we had passed Old Castle Point, the wind would be across the tide, we should have smoother water and might set the spinnaker. At this time we were the leading boat, but some-how or another Paddy Quennell sailed Tiny's boat ahead of us, although to leeward. This meant, that, for some strange reason, Tiny's boat went faster than the rest and that as soon as we had the opportunity, we had to put up the spinnaker to get on equal terms with her. So we started a little luffing to get them interested in this and to get into a position where our spinnaker would pay us better and while they were interested in luffing our masthead man nipped forward, put the spinnaker boom on the spinnaker and up she went. Just as it was up and set, a hell of a squall hit us and I had to use all my strength to keep the boat from broaching, for if she had brought this squall abeam with a spinnaker up she would certainly have filled and sank as there was nothing I could see we could do to save her from being blown over on to her beam ends. So away we chased to leeward of Paddy and quite soon we were abreast of him. Then the squall eased, but only for about thirty seconds, then down came another even harder one. We tore along with spray flying everywhere and everything strained to the utmost. So I decided that directly this squall had ended we would get the spinnaker down as it had done the job it was put up for, and that was to get us ahead of Paddy and I knew we would only have something like thirty seconds or so in which to get the spinnaker down between this and the next squall. With a good crew, however, this was no worry, and directly the squall eased, Michael nipped forward, unclipped the spinnaker off the fore end of the boom, while John gathered in to leeward and Reggie Bennett lowered it away, so we had it in the cabin in the twinkling of an eye and Michael could take his spinnaker boom off calmly and quietly – at least so it seemed after the wild rush we had with the spinnaker set. Even so, we had all the wind the boat wanted.

Now we started to luff up through to come out ahead of "Windflower" and to lead him round the Peel Bank buoy, but "Windflower's" superior speed stopped us doing this, so seeing that we would go round the buoy outside and under his lee, I bore right away so that I should be approaching the buoy on a close reach and would only have to luff up a little bit to get her right on to the wind and headed into Osborne Bay, while Paddy, approaching the buoy and having to turn at a very acute angle, would have no time to gather his sheets, and we could either go through his lee or to weather of him, whichever was best. Sure enough, they could not round too quickly and they left a gap of about twenty-five feet between them and the buoy with no chance at all of luffing in that weight of wind as even if they pointed the boat up, she would not go there, because of the windage in the mast and hull. So we darted through, just missing the buoy, well to windward, and the pair of us stood inshore to Osborne Bay, we gradually eating out to windward on the way in.

When in, both stood around on the port tack and up for the Old Castle Point, with Paddy some fifty yards astern. So we sailed, having to ease both the jib and the mainsheet in the heaviest of squalls to prevent the boat laying down on her beam ends and filling, for the squalls came down over the high lands of Osborne House, and flattened us out when they hit us.

Meantime, Dick Freemantle, steering "Margaret", No. 7, had stood round earlier under our lee and able to lay Castle Point, gained quite a bit on us, and so we arrived at Old Castle Point with the Poona in the lead, the Royal Corinthian next and the Royal London next, all of us, with only a half boat's length of water between us.

We all made a short one into the shore and then came about for the line and as we went along, Paddy Quennell in Tiny's boat decided to bear off to leeward, reach harder and go through our lee and I would dearly have loved to have borne away on top of him. The laws of sailing say that, while you can luff a man head to wind if he tries to pass you to windward, you should give him a free passage to leeward. So we held our course while Paddy slowly and surely sailed through our lee, and because the Starting Line and the Finishing Line points to the east a little, it meant that even if he was only abeam of us, he would get the gun first. So we came to the Finish with all the advantages in favour of Paddy, who had now pulled out with a clear wind to leeward.

I was sure that he was the winner, but we always live in hope, and arrived at shore to find that Paddy had won by one second, about a quarter of a boat's length, then the Royal London about four boat lengths astern and the Royal Yacht Squadron possibly a quarter of a mile astern of that.

So ended the day's racing with the Imperial Poona Yacht Club ahead on points.

We had a most enjoyable dinner after a bath at the Corinthian Yacht Club, and so to bed.

The following morn, I was awakened by a telephone call to say that a gale, force eight, was predicted for the day, and the postponement signal was hoisted, but by ten o'clock the owners of the boats had decided that the weather was not fit and so the Imperial Poona team settled down to some quiet drinks at eleven a.m., in my home. It was quite simple. Young Michael Ford, the measthead man, went for Madeira so all I had to do was to give him a glass and a bottle. Reggie decided on gin and sweet martini, and so he had two bottles, and John Chamier decided on the same thing, so he had two bottles, and I had my bottle of sherry, so we could all pour out our drinks as required and yarn about all sorts of things from my choir boy days to sailing on the day before.

Just before the sun was over the yard arm, we went along to the Corinthian Club to fill Prince Philip's Poona Pot – marvellous great tankard, beautiful to look at, to drink from, dating from George II, held two bottles of champagne comfortably. We filled the thing three times and then Tiny filled it with a wonderful mixture of vintage port and a wonderful old brandy. Both of them so mellow that they slid down like mother's milk and they were so potent that at dinner that night afterwards, Tiny complained that he had had no lunch, although he had had, to my knowledge, some wonderful beef, after melon, and finished with a great chunk of stilton cheese.

So ended the first races between the Clubs of Cowes.

After some recommendations for the following year, Uffa concludes:

These are my thoughts and also the story of the first series of races in the contest you have so brilliantly invented for us. I have never had so much fun sailing in any one day before and Bobby Lowein, who steered the Island Sailing Club's boat, came in for a drink this lunchtime on the Monday and he also said the same thing, and so we think that this new set of races will develop into the most important series of races in the country and possibly the world, and at the same time, be the greatest fun for all.

Thank you very much indeed for all the joy it has brought into the hearts of the twenty people who took part in it and also for the joy it has brought to Tiny Mitchell who is largely responsible for carrying out your ideas.

The event was clearly considered a success and repeated. The last placed club was responsible for organising the following year's races, so it was fortunate that Poona never lost, because the lack of a clubhouse or boats in the continent of Europe may have hindered proceedings somewhat.

The Island Sailing Club won in 1958 and 1959, but Poona was back victorious in 1960. The following year, the Royal London Yacht Club changed the event from fleet to match racing, with Prince Philip's approval, and the Royal Yacht Squadron won under this new format.

However, the Squadron's time at the top of the pile was short lived when they were last in 1962 and Poona victorious for the third time. Once again telegrams were exchanged:

To Buckingham Palace: *POONA WON POT BY ONE POINT.*

From Buckingham Palace: *FELICITATIONS. IF PRESSED WILL SEND SMALL TIN OF CURRY POWDER FOR CELEBRATION TIFFIN. COOCH PARWANI.*

However, this exchange of telegrams caused quite an episode as Reggie described in a letter to the palace:

I sent the telegram to Prince Philip before I left [on holiday], *little thinking that it would arouse such a hullabaloo indirectly as that which faced me on my return.*

I rang up the Postmaster to say he could start delivering letters again and he said that both he and the police had been trying to deliver a telegram they could not understand from someone they could not quite place but emanating from Buckingham Palace Post Office.

Poona was back in winning form in 1965 and won the event the following two years as well. With three victories in a row, Poona claimed that they had won the Cup outright and handed it back to the Maharaja who promptly represented it.

The original five clubs continued to compete in the event, with the losing club acting as host, until 1973 when it moved to Bembridge, was sailed in the club boats and expanded to involve all the sailing clubs based on the Isle of Wight and, of course, Poona.

The Poona Team at the Prince Philip Pot, 1970

Crew: Mike Ford, Nevill Ambler, Malcolm Green

RAIDS ON DEAUVILLE

In the 1960s, the Club was privileged to hoist the three balls up the mast of the Maharaja's yacht 'Bloodhound' and sail across the channel to the republic of France.

Before the first of these outings, a telegram was received by the yacht's Sailing Master at 6.30pm on 7th May 1964:

THE MAHARAJA OF COOCH PARWANI SENDS THE MEMBERS OF THE LOWER ORDERS OF THE IMPERIAL POONA YACHT CLUB AT PRESENT MORE OR LESS IN CHARGE OF BLOODHOUND A MESSAGE OF FEARFUL GREETINGS STOP HE CANNOT UNDERSTAND HOW BLOODHOUND GOT INTO THEIR HANDS AND HE PRAYS TO THE GOD SINKNOT THAT WHATEVER HAPPENS TO THE MEMBERS BLOODHOUND WILL RETURN SAFELY AFTER THIS HAZARDOUS EXPEDITION

Poona responded to such wishes in imperial style, as is detailed in the report written by Reggie:

BLOODHOUND TO DEAUVILLE
I.P.Y.C.
8 – 11 MAY 1964

There joined: *Commodore Bennett Sahib (Reggie Bennett)*
Baby Blake (Charles Blake)
Pilgrim Father (Mike Ford)
Yeti (Brian Appleton)
Sowar ke Batcha (Noel Dobbs)
Donkeyman (Malcolm Green)

As it was more or less blowing the roof off and the forecasters were predicting force 8 in all areas as a start, blowing up to forces 9-10 up north, discretion prevailed on Friday afternoon, 8th, and the sahibs contented themselves with erecting their yak-skin tents all over the ship. Brian Yeti had been given leave to arrive late, and by the time he arrived, about 7.30, the wind and the forecasters, and indeed the sahibs, were all considerably less windy and 'Bloodhound' proceeded immediately, logging 9.3 miles in the first hour from moorings in a rousing SW breeze that gave a close fetch on a course of 160° magnetic from Fort Blockhouse to Deauville west pierhead.

By midnight we were through the mid-Channel steamship lane, still logging over 9 knots. The efficacy of Bloodhound's navigation lights was simply demonstrated by the way the shipping scattered at our approach, even on a moonless night. We were going as fast as they were, anyway, which must have puzzled them.

In the small hours, as we entered the bay of the Seine, the wind dropped right away to a flat calm. Under all plain power 'Bloodhound' steamed into a cloudless sunny morning, picking up Havre L.V. at 0600 and squeaking through Deauville lock gates with only eight minutes to spare before closing time (of the lock, of course).

Squeaking is perhaps the wrong word so far as the sound is concerned, for Henri Millet, the Commodore of Deauville Y.C., and Pierre Faure Beaulieu, the Secretary, were lurking on the gate-side, wreathed in diabolical leers whose cause was soon to be revealed. A 'appy little belch, like, and there sailed up a couple of hundred feet a small black object which exploded with a stunning crash – a lifeboat maroon!

A series of these tremendous air-bursts helped us up-harbour, leaving Deauville quaking with fright. We moored up neatly with our stern to the Club itself, that elegantly converted 'blockaus' of the Organization Todt.

Now started the social whirl, 23 ½ hours of it. It may not have been original, but it was very nice to enjoy. An immediate visit to the club was soon superseded by an invitation to the Vice-President's villa at the other end of Deauville. Francis and John took watches, alternating as socialite and cookie. Francis was the socialite at lunch time.

As the hospitality asserted itself, the leers of the younger members became less inhibited and so did their French language. All hands were capable of quite a good stream before the day was over.

After luncheon on board, hands enjoyed a fairly lengthy zizzex on deck in the sun but the afternoon was enlivened by a visit from a solemn young Customs officer who came to inspect the ship's passport, a new idea. There were a few questions to be answered and the sahibs gathered to help him. Ship's name? Difficult to spell in French but could be done. Owner? We looked at one another and told him. "La Reine d'Angleterre?" "That's right." Next question – Age? Ship's Age of Construction? No, age of the proprietaire. Such an un-Sahib-like question got no very clear answer, and suddenly the officer picked up his papers and started off ashore, asserting, "Ce n'est pas un rigolade ...." etc. etc. etc. as it all faded into the distance. We had pressed Lloyds Register, duly engraved, upon him to no avail. He made two later rather incoherent and excited visits before somebody in his office must have told him – as nobody on the club quay seemed prepared to do. They weren't going to spoil the fun!

The evening held a Yacht Club reception at 6.30 and a reception at the Casino at 10. But we anticipated and asked the Club officers and other old friends aboard at 5.45, as they were dying to come. The Sous-Prefet from Lisieux, and the Mayor and Contesse d'Ornano came too – she remembered our Pilgrim Father when 'Mayflower' arrived in America, so Mike Ford was a bit above himself for the rest of the evening. This very attractive mayoress and her husband spoke English with ease, as did about half the members, so, apart from a speech of welcome from Max Boiteau, the Club President, and a reply in the Commodore Sahib's best fractured French and Hindustani, communications were easy.

Dinner on board (Francis' turn) was enlivened by a few light-hearted somersaults by the Baby Blake who had earlier delighted the French by appearing in his formal topee and other regalia. Then to the final "champagne d'honneur" at the Casino, given by Jacques Gilbert, the Directeur. Here, in the absence of some of the distractions during the earlier proceedings, the Sahibs turned their attention to the tables and the other distractions surrounding these.

On Sunday morning, after some final purchases of postcards, croissants and other consumable stores, the Sahibs bade farewell to the D.Y.C.'s braves and proceeded to sea at 9.30, with one final and highly un-sabbatarian conclusion. A weak cold front had cleared the sky and left a light breeze in NW, of all places! So we slowly stood out past Le Havre on port tack and settled down to a whole day's flat calm and basking some 10 miles north of Havre. An engine run across Channel brought us into the next gathering warm front, and Bloodhound stormed in from the Owers at a good 10 knots with mizzen staysail set, mooring up just before 5 a.m. on Monday.

The operation, ambitious as it was, went without a hitch and must have given greater pleasure to more participants than any but a few of its kind. The atmosphere on board was quite delightful. The gratitude of the Sahibs knows no bounds and is most emphatically and even violently expressed. It was a huge privilege and a great joy. We would like to give something to the ship to express our feelings – but she is so beautifully found that it is difficult to think of anything not actually useless. We shall hope to be able to entertain the gallant Sailing Master to tiffin in due course, and meanwhile we should like to express to our Maharaja and to his Maharanee our delightful thanks for the treat they have given us.

It may seem odd, but among the remarkably Imperial thinkers of Deauville it does seem that a Republican Cell may well have been started by the visit of a Royal Yacht.

Another raid on Deauville was made in 1967, although Reggie Bennett was not present. The third trip was the last voyage made by 'Bloodhound' before she was disposed of by her owners. It also marked the foundation of another Outpost of the Club.

It is clearly important that the report of a trip with such dual historical importance is recorded in full:

I.P.Y.C BLOODHOUND TO DEAUVILLE
$10^{th}/13^{th}$ October, 1969.

The last cruise of Bloodhound was by a felicitous coincidence allotted to the Imperial Poona Yacht Club, at least Poona thinks it was felicitous. No less than nine Sahibs were accommodated, "hot bunk" principle; This was found acceptable in the absence of the Haro-bhoi (Rule 18).

The Sahibs were led by the Commode, Baby Blake and Mike Ford (Pilgrim Father) as watchkeepers, together with Brian Appleton (Yeti or Abominable Snowman), Noel Dobbs (Sowar Ke Batcha), Peter Hunter (Babun), Malcolm Green (Donkeyman), Johnsons Wooderson (Ramm of Kutch) and Nevill Ambler (Chapatty).

This allowed three watches of three, in three-hour watches, and proved a most agreeable arrangement while David Gay, Mike and Paul were able to be idlers (although not especially idle!).

I joined the ship about 12.30 on Friday and Baby Blake and I were hardly even outside our first gin when a blanket of fog, such as had been investing the Home Counties since dawn, suddenly rolled up and enveloped us. No half measures. It was there to stay. All hands joined, however, in some miraculous way and at 3.00 p.m. we slipped and proceeded.

We had seen the last of terra firma. We saw neither side as we left harbour and we only dimly saw the Isle of Wight boat as it crept in through the Spring ebb. We whirled merrily down the Channel skipping from buoy to buoy while the fog dripped heavily down the back-stays and soaked everybody. We even had to rig a dodger on the pulpit to try and keep our forward lookout dry as he stood up there with the sparklet hooter. The last buoy we saw was Warner and soon even the sun was obscured as the fog bank thickened. This remained so until the approach of evening when the sun gradually began to be seen at a much lower angle of sight and finally our radius of vision began to increase as darkness began to fall. We motored merrily on with the Poona flag blowing out bravely in the floodlight at the masthead. A light easterly air got up as the fog thinned and we were able to keep the mainsail and jib full, this adding a knot to our speed.

The night watches were fortunately pretty clear and in the Middle not one ship was sighted. Towards morning the engine was stopped for a while and the ship was making over five knots with the sails just nicely free. As dawn came up at about 6.00 a.m., Le Havre lightship was sighted, only to vanish suddenly when about a 100 degrees off as thick fog came down again. This continued throughout our approach to the land but we picked up the Fairway buoy for Deauville and felt our way inshore, while the bleat of the foghorn boomed round the horizon to mislead us. By and by we saw that the sea appeared to be streaming in the chilly atmosphere and leads began to show through the banks along to port, a rift in the bank suddenly disclosed the roof of the Normandy Hotel which was instantly recognised by the more experienced hands. The kedge was dropped forthwith and breakfast was served at 8.30.

We entered harbour at 09.30 in clear air and a light southerly breeze, announcing our arrival with a feu-de-joy from our large mortar on the foredeck with coloured star shell. We were berthed alongside the club house where we divided our attention between hygiene and Ricard.

The Deauville Yacht Club had been specially reopened for us and Madame Lucien had even returned from the South of France to dispense to us. Commodore Henry Millet, the Mayor of the nearby metropolis of Blonville, duly received us together with a number of his hospitable colleagues shortly to be enrolled in this Section Batard Normand. M. Miguet, the Sous Prefet from Lisieux, another prospective member of the Section visited the ship with his wife, and Johnson Wooderson's shifting into shore-going clothes was much admired. Nevill Ambler met again two ladies who had been introduced to him on a previous visit as marriageable playmates, until he visited their homes and met their husbands and numerous families. These ladies, Madame Pruvost and Madame Martinache, were indeed the life and soul of the party at all times. It need only be said that their husbands were present so that such people as Hunter were restrained to some extent.

In the evening Commodore Millet and the Club entertained Bloodhound to a delightful little Champagne party at which of course many of the Poonas as well as the Bloodhound were meeting old friends from earlier visits or from earlier contests.

The party adjourned to the nearby Ocean Hotel, where Charlie Blake had set himself up in splendour, and nineteen people sat down to a very fine cous-cous which just about knocked everybody out. It is regrettable to have to report that Brian Appleton was laid low with a stomach upset apparently deriving from his original upset at Zermatt some years ago, but it is equally regrettable that Charlie Blake's topee proved not to be waterproof, to the detriment of Suzanne Millet who was sitting alongside him; that Malcolm Green played a highly successful

57

custard-pie act at Peter Hunter's expense, and that Peter Hunter chose to entertain the assembled company from the middle of the table with a song and story, in what can only be described as his appalling taste. It was all the more unfortunate that in the restaurant there was a gentleman from Paris who had come to Deauville for a quiet weekend away from his wife and family and was dining alone and communing with his own spirit. He did not have much of a chance against the enthusiastic expressions of sympathy showered upon him, which were no more helpful than Hunter's somewhat off colour performance. The evening ended at a discotheque nearby in the heat and almost total darkness lit from time to time by the fluorescent brilliance of the chef's tall hat worn by Commodore Millet in the light of the ultra-violet transmitters. A toast was proposed by Henry Millet to the Queen-Empress, to which I responded with a toast to the President of France and "L' empereur en retraite".

Next morning Charlie Blake entertained all hands to breakfast at the Ocean Hotel, which had also been opened especially for the occasion of our visit. After a short visit to the town for a little shopping, the Sahibs assembled on board at 11.00 to receive their French friends.

It was a cool and brightly sunny morning with the same light easterly air, and Bloodhound's deck was soon fully occupied by a party. Among the further Deauvillains were the monstrous Pierre Lepeudry, that particularly dangerous helmsman Pierre Frottie and young Jean-Pierre Millet, who on hearing of our arrival had come up from Paris specially this morning. It was a splendid concourse of people, very largely old friends and almost entirely the prospective members of the Section Batard Normand, which was hereby inaugurated. The title is of course the reference to a Duke, whose parentage has always been impuned by history, who lived a mile or two from Deauville and gate crashed his way into England in 1066. No reflection is intended on any other Dukes or indeed on any other Normans!

The foundation membership of the Section comprises:

> *Sous-Prefet R. Miguet*
> *Commodore Henry Millet*
> *Pierre Frottie*
> *Pierre Lepeudry*
> *M. Martinache*
> *M. Pruvost*
> *Jean-Pierre Millet*

all of whom were present, together with the Depute et Maire of Deauville, Michel d'Ornano, the President of the D.Y.C., Maitre Max Boiteau, and the secretary of the D.Y.C. Pierre Faure-Beaulieu, which last three were unable to be present.

58

It was decided to try and hold a tiffin in London in late November if possible and one at the Sous-Prefecture at Lisieux next Easter.

Now the party began to break up. Commodore Millet and one or two others had guests coming to lunch, but the remainder, particularly the girls, were retained on board while the ship let go of the quay and proceeded out of the basin before the tide should neap her on the way out. The signal for departure was a series of thunderous explosions from the mortars and maroons at the Club House, together with the end-of-commission expenditure of pyrotechnic stores, being particularly admired, and the red smoke generators making it almost impossible for David Gay to find the hole in the granite from which to head for the open sea, the following wind keeping the smoke clouds accurately over the ship.

No incidents are to be reported with the customs or any other services on this visit, and so no repercussions need to be expected from this direction on this occasion.

Bloodhound kedged to seaward of the pierhead and the party continued. As the champagne began to run low, however, parties of our guests began to be put ashore together with the last of the glasses borrowed from the Club.

A somewhat carefree lunch was taken on deck in the sunshine, Charlie Blake still in his full rig and Hunter as usual disgracing himself with the brandy.

At 14.45 the mainsail was hoisted and the kedge recovered and the great downhill rush across the Channel began, with the Genoa boomed out to starboard and a very healthy breeze going, so speeds were from seven to nine knots and more throughout the afternoon, evening and night. The Owers was sighted at 01.00, Bembridge Ledge was abeam at 04.00 and at 05.55 Bloodhound ran herself firmly on the putty less than a length from her berth in the Cold-harbour. The Sahibs dispersed and Bloodhound herself prepared for her slipping and survey at the end of the most glorious end to a most fabulous career.

It must be claimed that the end surpassed any possible glories at any other time, and to say that the Sahibs are grateful is a woeful understatement. They hurl themselves prostrate, heaving loads of dust and ashes over themselves in their expressions of gratitude to the owners, for being so generous and indeed so trusting as to allow so precious a ship into the hands of such an unprincipled gang of villains.

BACK IN BLIGHTY

The previous two chapters have shown the Imperial Poona Yacht Club in rude health in the 1960s, often ruling the waves in Cowes and possibly waiving the rules in Deauville (certainly according to the hard pressed custom's official!). This state of activity continued into the 1970s, although the Club had to do its irreverent bit to keep up with the times.

Rule Changes

The introduction of the Race Relations Acts 1964-70 resulted in an additional clause in the Club's rules: *"For 'white' read 'black' and for 'coloured' read 'coloured' throughout."*

Voting for the Flag Officers was so tight in 1970 that, instead of just a Great White Vice, an additional post of Great Black Vice was also created, again acknowledging the recent legislation.

Further legislation in 1978 (and anticipating more) required another change (as is stated in the Club's rules) *"in order to conform to the relevant legislation, to wit the Abolition of Sex Differentiation Act 1978, the Parthenogenesis Act 1979, the Androgyny Act 1980 and the Universal Hermaphroditism Act 1984: Rule 6, last sentence, shall be deemed to read 'No memsahib, male or female, is eligible'."*

Fractured Spar

A regular contest against the Flying Fifteen fleet at the newly-founded Grafham Water Sailing Club was introduced in April 1967, and the Fractured Spar trophy was sailed for on many occasions in the late 1960s and early 1970s. This explains the Poona flag in the bar of that land-locked club.

40th Anniversary Tiffin

For the Club's 40th anniversary, in 1974, members were privileged to be invited for a Tiffin onboard the Maharaja's Imperial Dhow, Britannia, on Sunday 4th August 1974 during Cowes Week.

While Poona could be accused of many things, being ostentatious is perhaps not one of them – it is quite possibly the only club where an invitation to such a special dinner could be sent out by the club's secretary in a hand written and photocopied note!

But the sahibs responded and had a magnificent evening.

By this time, Uffa Fox, who had been the Maharaja's sailing companion during Cowes Week for many years, had died and Reggie

Bennett had taken his place in this role, regularly staying on board for the week.

Abdul Gunneybags

Perhaps as a result of word of this honoured occasion reaching the back streets of the sub-continent, in March 1975, Reggie received certain documents from an immigrant from Bombay which appeared to be a request for membership from someone called Abdul Gunneybags, who claimed to be a Bandari Wallah (with much acclaim for his curry and samoosas) as well as having sea experience.

Enclosed with this begging letter were what can only be described as a sheaf of spurious references to his skills as a cook / bearer from previous employers in Bombay.

However, despite all this, when his possible candidature was circulated to the members, no black topees were received. Indeed, the Great Gorgeous Rear, John Chamier, replied with some support to his application, writing *"he has a yacht aboard which he got lost and since it only sails against the sun he was forced to go on till he got back."* He was, of course, the first person to do this single-handed and non-stop.

His election was approved, but not without serious reservations from the Maharaja, who described him as a *"miserable sea cook"*! Nevertheless, Abdul, with tales of his time in India, and bottle of lime pickle, is always an entertaining participant at any Tiffin, often in partnership with the Serang, Nevill Ambler, who can also recount tales of the sub-continent.

Poona And The SINS

Abdul's election was just in time, because that summer there was the London Festival of Sail and he, under his slightly more conventional name of Robin Knox-Johnston, happened to be manager of the St. Katherine's Yacht Haven.

He organised a match, on Wednesday 27th August 1975, between the fourty year old Imperial Poona Yacht Club and a recently formed group who called themselves the SINS. This stood for the Society of International Nautical Scribes. This event was described in the Peterborough column of The Daily Telegraph as *"without question the oddest event during the Port of London Clipper Regatta."*

As one would expect from the groups concerned, and Abdul's involvement, the rules for this event contained some entertaining elements:

The starting signals: *A topee will be held aloft at the five minute signal, and will be lowered for the start roughly in time with the start signal. If these two signals do not coincide, discretion may be used as to which start signal is used, subject to the Race Officer not changing his mind afterwards.*

The scoring system: *The IPYC shall be deemed to be the winners unless the protest committee decide otherwise upon receipt of a properly phrased protest which should include suitably compelling evidence and a protest fee of 8 Annas.*

Penalty points: *In the event of arrest of any of the competitors, each team shall be responsible for bail of its own members.*

The report of the event in Yachts & Yachting (which is reprinted with their kind permission) read:

Two Lasers per side were used, the race was a relay and the course was a figure of eight around the bascules of Tower Bridge. It has to be recorded that the Harbour Master and River Police were very tolerant of the whole affair, incredulous as they were of the persistence of a constant stream of different helmsmen in widely varying attire making repeated passes at the traffic in the London River's main fairway.

The SINS team, having scored a resounding conquest, were declared the victors – despite a clause in the racing instructions which stated clearly that the Poona should be declared the winners. The latter, it was suspected, had wind of the fact that the first prize was a bottle of White Horse whisky, albeit a very large one, while second prize was a crate of bubbly.

Jubilee River Pageant and Fireworks

The following year the Queen Empress celebrated her Golden Jubilee and it was felt appropriate that Poona marked this occasion. There was nowhere better to do this than at the heart of government.

Poona was not alone in this gathering, organised by Reggie – they were joined by members of the Royal Thames Yacht Club and the House of Commons Yacht Club. However, their presence on the House of Commons' terrace was not approved of by all, as the Guardian recorded on 11th June 1976, and is reproduced here with their kind permission:

Damp MPs lose their berth right
By Simon Hoggart, Political Correspondent

A number of MPs were more than a little disgruntled yesterday after finding themselves displaced from marquees on the hallowed ground of the Commons terrace for the Jubilee firework display.

They could stand on the terrace itself on Thursday night in the drizzle, but the long, gaily striped marquees were occupied by about 500 well-off yachtsmen from four different clubs who had been booked for some weeks.

The booking had been made by Dr Reginald Bennett, the Tory MP for Fareham, who is chairman of the catering sub-committee at the Commons. Dr Bennett, an enthusiastic yachtsmen, belongs to two of the clubs and is commodore of one of them, the Imperial Poona Yacht Club. The yachtsmen paid for the use of the terrace; the money would go into House of Commons funds.

The result was that the MPs stood clutching what drink they could find and braving the rain while the water pageant went past and the fireworks went up. Not surprisingly, it was Labour MPs who were most angered by the sight of the yachtsmen. Mr Arthur Latham, a former chairman of the Tribune group, says he will table a Commons motion protesting about "these high class squatters taking over the Palace of Westminster."

Mr Latham went on: "MPs and their guests could not even get a cup of tea because the catering committee had let out accommodation to these clubs. We stood in the rain while the marquees were handed over to these people, suitably furnished with a bar and booth. If we had been displaced by people like pensioners we would not have minded, but to let it out to the most undesirable elements of British Society is too much to stomach."

Raid To Deauville

A fourth raid to Deauville took place in 1976, on board the newly elected John Prentice's 'Battlecry'. It was reported that:

The natives were again friendly, and have proclaimed that in light of these four cultural missions, to say nothing of the occupation of the Pegasus Bridge over the Orne some time before, Normandy, and in particular, Calvados, have returned to the Imperial fold. Cognac and Bordeaux have not yet been reinstated, but efforts will continue.

Prince Philip Pot

We left the Prince Philip Cup in an earlier chapter when it moved to Bembridge in 1973 and expanded to be a championship in keelboats for the twelve sailing clubs based in the Isle of Wight (including Poona).

Poona was not successful in the first year of the new format, but was in 1974. The following year, with only two races held due to strong winds, there was an unbreakable tie for first place between Poona and the Royal Corinthian Yacht Club. The donor commented *"with pots, as with wits, it is better to have half than none."*

Poona was next victorious in 1980.

With the demise of the Bembridge club boats, Noel Dobbs (McPuke) negotiated the transfer of the event to Seaview in 1990, sailed in their Mermaids. In the first year at Seaview, 8 teams competed and Poona won their 10th victory since 1957. This was added to two years later in 1992.

Poona has always strived to maintain the traditions of this unique competition (although it could hardly claim to have become *"the most important series of races in the world"* which Uffa Fox anticipated after the first event). Seaview continue to host the event, and Poona's Peter Hunter has become the Race Officer and ensures the traditions and purpose of the event are upheld.

Sir Hugh Janion

At the end of a successful naval career, Rear-Admiral Sir Hugh Janion was Captain of HM Yacht Britannia for the unusually long period from 1975 to 1981. In this position he got to know Reggie and it was entirely appropriate that he was elected a member of Poona on his retirement, with the title, Colonel-in-Chief, and the name, Sam Pan, Captain of the Heads.

His first role in "civvy street" was when he was asked by the Prince of Wales to handle his wedding presents. An obituary for Hugh recounted:

He had to take on four assistants and eventually sent letters of thanks to the donors of about 6,000 gifts, stored in the cinema of Buckingham Palace, ranging from a solid gold dhow to a book entitled 'Mining in Botswana', and from a heart shaped potato to a Clementi piano.

What this account does not mention is the letter which appeared on his desk from Motilai Banerji Ram, the humble secretary of the Indio-Pakistani Youth Clubs (IPYC) in Peckham and Brixton offering either a Tandori oven or ghari with wheels.

When he realised who this was actually from, Hugh replied that the royal couple would be delighted to accept either gift, but then he got the reply:

Is saddest and ashaming happening destruction of oven for tandoori, alas all bricks stolen and throwing at Constabulary when humble secretariat not looking, also gharri altogether burned up and wheels thrown away by untouchable Harijans from Bangladesh or Peckham extra sadness indeed very sorry.

A few years later, in 1984 (which we will come to soon), Hugh returned to Britannia, drawing from the stores a pair of bell-bottoms and a flannel, a mop and a bucket, which he returned a few days later. This mystified the crew, but history records him in a photograph at the Poona Jubilee, sitting in the front row, equipped as Captain of the Heads, surmounted by a great wide conical Shan State straw hat.

Seaview Buffs

In 1978 the Seaview Buffs, an "inner circle" of the Seaview Yacht Club which is even older than Poona but with a very similar constitution and comparable behaviour, challenged Poona to a match in Mermaids.

This has been repeated ever since and the Thunder Mug is presented to each club alternatively at this match.

This is now the main Poona sailing gathering of the year and consists of a very good dinner on the Saturday night and racing on the Sunday. Not surprisingly, it is an occasion of much merry making and one or two incidents. The author will be accused of censorship if he fails to provide details of one such incident which has become part of Poona folklore.

Allegedly, when the Poona party were walking home after dinner from the club to Peter Hunter's house, a certain person was spotted by the local constabulary relieving himself on the wheel of a parked Seaview bus.

The party then proceeded down the garden path and turned right into the house. However, after a short while, there was a knock on the door. Peter Andreae opened it to find the local bobby demanding to speak to the last person who entered the house. Quick as a flash, Peter said he would willingly collect the said person, who was none other than Rear-Admiral Sir Hugh Janion, late of the Royal Yacht Britannia.

Hugh's experience in dealing with the lower ranks came to the fore as, complete with monocle and dressed in his monogrammed silk dressing gown, he dismissed the constable.

Allegedly, no Poona member lied during this incident, as the last member of the party walking down the path (the Gully Gully Man) had failed to turn right into the house, but had collapsed to the left and was fast asleep in the flowerbed! This left the more respectable, and less inebriated, Sir Hugh as the last person to have entered the house.

Tiffins

Regular Tiffins continued during the 1970s, usually held in London at White's in St James's, but Reggie's knighthood in 1979 demanded a greater celebration. This was held during Cowes Week in the, appropriately named, Durbar Room at Osborne House on the Isle of Wight. This also marked the Club's 45th anniversary. The club returned to the same venue for a Durbar in 1990.

Another notable Durbar was the celebration of the Club's half century in 1984. Sadly someone with celestial authority had left their mark a bit earlier and grabbed the actual anniversary date, 22nd April, as Easter Sunday, so Poona (unusually) held back and celebrated the following weekend.

Durbar Celebrating The Imperial Poona Yacht Club's Golden Jubilee Moundsmere Manor, 27th April, 1984

It was a grand affair at Moundsmere Manor, near Basingstoke, home of Mark Andreae, Fuzzy Wuzzy, who was promptly re-named Cornucopia as a result of his magnificence.

Reggie's invitation promised *"unlimited sherbet and a spectrum of more or less inflammatory curries, together with ghee, dhal, poppadums, chapatti, Bombay Duck and other fauna and flora, at a modest charge not exceeding one lakh of rupees per turban."*

This Durbar was attended by most of the active sahibs, accompanied by memsahibs and camp followers, representatives of many of the overseas outposts and those who had previously been on the active list who were still active enough to attend. Most were, as requested, in oriental dress or yellow and red attire. We have already described Hugh Janion's costume.

An Outpouring Of Outposts

The Home station was beaten to it, by a new outpost, the Middle Kingdom Outpost, or Middle Kingdom Mandarins, which was formed on 22nd April 1984 and had its Inaugural Tiffin at the Royal Hong Kong Yacht Club on the precise day of anniversary.

They were fortunate enough to be entertained to a Tiffin on board Britannia by the Maharaja when he visited Hong Kong in 1987.

Not content with such high honour, the Middle Kingdom outpost also started missionary work. One of its sahibs, Roland Lennox King, moved to New Zealand and found companionship with James Watlington, from the Bermuda outpost, as their new home hosted the America's Cup competition. With Reggie's blessing, on 9th February 1997, they formed the Inverted Colonies Outpost in 1997.

The Club burgee was duly *"hung from the wall not two fathoms from and facing down upon the great Silver Mug."*

Endeavour

1989 saw the renovation of the J-Class yacht Endeavour by Elizabeth Meyer. Involved in this re-fit was Poona member, Riggah, Frank Murdoch. Frank was responsible for the revolutionary rod-rigging, as well as many other unique sailing aids, when this yacht was competing for the Americas Cup back in 1934, and his knowledge was invaluable for the renovation.

He engineered an invitation for the Imperial Poona Yacht Club to sail onboard this magnificent re-launched yacht on 7th July 1989. With a 130ft yacht there was room for the entire Poona membership on the trip, although the author was prevented from attending by the birth of his first child.

Reggie recalls *"beating down past Calshot with the double-clawed jib-topsail set was a stirring experience."* However, there was something missing – the Poona members needed refreshment if this was to be a really memorable Tiffin. Fortunately, a radio message from Hamish Janson (Oont) to the Royal Yacht Squadron saw that club's launch – suitably supplied – rendezvous with Endeavour mid-Solent, and the problem was solved.

I wish I had been there!

The Champagne Arrives For Poona's Outing On Endeavour, 7th July, 1989

More Tiffins

Throughout the 1990s regular Tiffins continued, and the 60th anniversary (1994) was celebrated by a Tiffin at the house of Peter Andreae, Grand Mufti and Finance Member. No less than eleven far-flung representatives of the imperial outposts were present.

In 1997 a Glorious Durbar was held in April at the recently renovated Frogmore House, a Bungalow chosen by the Queen Empress Victoria in which to enjoy her honeymoon. It stands in the grounds of Windsor Castle.

The Maharaja warmly welcomed us, although the staff were later heard to say that they had wished someone had warned them it was a piss-up. They had to go back to the castle three times for more drink!

68

The Durbar at Frogmore House, Windsor Castle, April 1997

West Country Tour

In 1999, Poona went further and toured the West Country. This involved no less than twelve of the twenty one sahibs considered active at the time, accompanied by memsahibs and camp followers.

The first stop was at Fowey, where we competed against the Troy Class, sailing from the Fowey Gallants Sailing Club. That evening, a Tiffin was organised at the Royal Fowey Yacht Club from whence to bed.

The next morning we travelled to Falmouth where the intention was to race against the sublimely named Falmouth Artisan's River Training Squadron (FARTS, for short) in the classic working oyster-boats of the Truro River. Sadly, the tides did not co-operate, and so we dined at The Ganges Restaurant at Mylor instead.

That afternoon we travelled to the Pendennis Yard in Falmouth to see the Commode's old ship, Shamrock V, which had just arrived for a re-fit. Reggie was clearly in his element as he checked out his old boat from over sixty years previously, recalling the uneven deck and other details.

THE NEW MILLENIUM

The Founder Dies

The last Tiffin Reggie attended was on 26th July 2000 at Whites, in the presence of the Maharaja. Sadly in September 2000 Reggie became ill and was admitted to Charing Cross Hospital. After two and a half months he moved to a nursing home in part of what was once the Royal Masonic Hospital at Hammersmith.

Despite being very ill, weak, and mentally confused, Reggie had not stopped thinking imperially and was concerned about the future of the Imperial Poona Yacht Club. He made several attempts to write to the Maharaja about the continuation of the Club, but finally it was left to Henrietta, Reggie's wife, to write to this effect. He wanted the Maharaja to help select a new Commode.

Reggie died on 19th December 2000 and this was greeted with great sadness by both the sailing and political communities. This history started with his obituary, and it is not necessary to report all the tributes, but Ian Wooldridge's words in the Daily Mail are worth recording:

Arrivederci, Reggie
A lovely, irreplaceable character died this week and I write with great respect of Reggie Bennett, more formally known for 24 years as Sir Reginald Bennett MP.

He portrayed all his austere Wykehamist education by hugely enjoying yachting, long lunches and public life, roughly in that order.

He was wonderful company and had packed in about 150 years of life before his death at the age on 89.

Picking Up The Pieces

Peter Hunter, the Great White Vice, was at home when the phone rang and the voice at the other end informed him they were calling from Buckingham Palace. He nearly replied that he was the Queen of Sheeba when it became clear that the Maharaja was fulfilling Reggie's wishes and urging Poona to continue and elect a replacement for him

A Tiffin was held in April 2001 at the Royal Thames Yacht Club and the future was much discussed. Should Reggie's resignation under Rule 9 (a) [death] be refused, as had been the case for The Commodore of the Repulsive But Not Revolting Outpost, Bill Gooderham?

In the end, it was decided to elect Reggie as the Celestial Commode and Peter Hunter would become the Terrestrial Commode.

(Because of Hunter's appalling spelling, this was initially written as Terrestial Commode, but fortunately this was corrected by Buckingham Palace!). Malcolm Green was elevated from Great Gorgeous Rear to Great White Vice, and Ben Vines was elected Great Gorgeous Rear.

The Poona Team at Seaview in 2007

New Blood

Ben Vines was part of a group of young sailors who Reggie had prompted the Club to elect after the 50th anniversary. These included Ben, Andrew Green and Ed Smith who had all been in the British Universities' Sailing Team which had toured the United States in 1995.

Their election was felt to *"greatly increase the credibility of the Poona Teams in world-class events such as the Prince Philip Pot, and will be able to represent Poona in events far and wide."*

Their election, and that of other younger members, soon had the anticipated effect, winning the Prince Philip Pot in 1998, 1999, 2002, 2003, 2004 and 2005.

Andrew Green also became very active on the Match Racing circuit and won the Royal Bermuda Yacht Club's Gold Cup for Poona in 1999 – the first time for 40 years it had been in English hands.

A Poona team also started entering major team racing events, in 2004 reaching the quarter finals of the Wilson Trophy.

Not So Young Blood

But the younger members of the club did not grab all the sailing headlines for Poona. In 2006 Abdul Gunneybags set out on his second solo round the world trip, this time stopping, in his boat, who's Poona name was Sagah In-Shore Ranse, competing in the Velux 5 Oceans Race.

He received a message shortly before the start of the race:

Now to Abdul we cheer,
As we down a large beer,
While Sagah sets her sails,
With a man hard as nails,
And Hot Chilli Sauce,
To complete his resource,
So we sing to the skies
As the ocean he flies:

The sons of the Prophet are brave men and bold
And quite unaccustomed to fear,
But the bravest by far in the ranks of the Shah,
Was Abdul Abulbul Amir.

If you wanted a man to encourage the van,
Or harass the foe from the rear,
Storm fort or redoubt, you had only to shout
For Abdul Abulbul Amir.

Salaams and Salutations, may the Great Gods bless you,
From the Massed Ranks of POONA Sahibs.

Robin finished third in this race – a great achievement for someone 67 years young!

Tiffins

While Reggie's presence always guaranteed a good party, his absence has not prevented Poona from continuing to have them.

At the Regatta in 2001 to celebrate the 150th anniversary of the first Americas Cup race in Cowes, a memorable Tiffin was held at the Irrigation Fellah's house in Cowes, attended by the Maharaja.

Regular Tiffins are held during Cowes Week, often at John Terry's Commodore's House, and in 2008 the Maharaja invited the sahibs to drinks on board THV Galatea, the new Trinity House Vessel.

In March 2006 there was a Tiffin at the Royal Thames Yacht Club to celebrate 50th anniversary of Prince Philip Pot, with the donor present.

And So To 75 Years

This book is published as Poona celebrates the 75th anniversary of its founding. Not bad for a Club which was actually disbanded after four years because "*it had served its purpose.*"

A hint of the reason for its longevity was provided in the newspaper article about the first races against the Revolting Colonists in 1951: "*The reason for it has gone, but the spirit and comradeship have survived.*"

It is a totally unique club, with a limited, but surprisingly diverse, membership, who enjoy each other's company.

It is undoubtedly true that, without Reggie, it has lost his magic. People also have less time available now for the more frivolous things in life, and, with only twenty five members, events need well over half of them attending, which is not easily achieved. But when they do happen, the magic returns and some members are even capable of speech, as the rules say they may be!

Chota Hazri!

FLAG OFFICERS

Commodore

1934-38	Sir Archibald Hope	1946-2000	Sir Reginald Bennett

Celestial Commode

2001-	Sir Reginald Bennett

Terrestrial Commode

2001-	Peter Hunter

Great White Vice

1934-38	Charles Johnston	1998-2001	Peter Hunter
1946-70	Sir Heneage Ogilvie	2001-	Prof Sir Malcolm Green
1970-82	Charles Blake		
1982-98	Brian Appleton		

Great Black Vice

1970-81	Stephen Longsdon

Great Gorgeous Rear

1934-38	Roy Mitchell	1982-98	Peter Hunter
1946-49	Stephen Longsdon	1998-2001	Malcolm Green
1949-55	John Palmer	2001-	Ben Vines
1955-82	John Chamier		

Colonel-in-Chief

1934-62	Tiny Mitchell	1991-94	Rear Admiral Sir Hugh Janion
1968-70	Sir Heneage Ogilvie		
1973-90	Sir Alec Rose		

Secretariat-Wallah

1934	J H M Rabone	1949-66	Hugh Somerville
1934-36	Arthur Whitehead	1966-67	Stephen Longsdon
1946	Reggie Bennett	1968	Peter Andreae
1946-47	Cecil Knight	1969-74	Nevill Ambler
1947-49	John Dunn	1974-	Prof Sir Malcolm Green
1949	Reggie Bennett		

75 YEARS OF
PORT & BALLS

The histories of two unique sailing clubs

By the same author:

A Hundred Years of Sailing at Oxford University (1984)
25 More Years of Sailing at Oxford University (2009)

75 YEARS OF
PORT & BALLS

THE HISTORIES OF THE

OXFORD & CAMBRIDGE
SAILING SOCIETY

&

IMPERIAL POONA
YACHT CLUB

By Jeremy Atkins

First published, February 2009.
By Jeremy Atkins, Thorn Villa, Thorn Way, Long Itchington, Southam, Warwickshire. CV47 9PF.

ISBN 978-0-9509179-2-4

A CIP catalogue record for this book is available from the British Library.

Printed in the UK by the MPG Books Group.

INTRODUCTION

The President of the Oxford & Cambridge Sailing Society, Andrew Reid, asked me to write a history of the Society to mark the 75th anniversary of its founding in 1934.

As a member, and past Secretary, of this Club it was a privilege to accept such a commission. However, I am also a member of the Imperial Poona Yacht Club, which was formed just two months after the Oxford & Cambridge Sailing Society and, in some ways, in response to it.

Whilst both clubs have distinguished themselves separately, they have many common elements. Both were founded in 1934 by eminent Oxbridge yachtsmen, both were led by strong characters, and largely adopted their personality, and both are now evolving in the period after the death of their main founder.

I therefore expanded the commission to cover both clubs. The Society's history is, rightly, the lead story in this publication and the Poona history appears back to front, for Poona is famous for doing things backwards.

The title for the book comes from other famous characteristics of each club:

- The Society, while primarily focussed on the sailing sport of team racing, has managed to build, maintain and enjoy an impressive cellar of port over the years.
- Poona, whose burgee consists of three red balls on a yellow background, is often described as "a load of balls".

So here we are – 75 years of port and balls, and a lot of other things. Formed as foes, but now bound together in a book!

I hope you enjoy the read as much as I have enjoyed writing it.

Jeremy Atkins

Each history starts with an obituary of the respective Club's main personality and driving force. These are reproduced from the Independent newspaper. There are some historical inaccuracies in both, but they are reproduced in this book exactly as they were originally published.

ACKNOWLEDGEMENTS

The task of writing the Society's history has been made relatively easy by the fact that the Minute Books, newsletters and correspondence are virtually intact since the formation of the Club. In particular, Stewart Morris, who was Secretary for 32 years, was an avid chronicler, tirelessly recording the minutes of the meetings in his fair hand.

I would like to put on record my gratitude to all the Secretaries of the Society that have followed Stewart, and who have, by and large, maintained excellent records which has made my role more of an editor than an author.

On the Poona side, Reggie Bennett also kept impressive records, including a Minute Book till the early 1950s, and a stack of photographs which have allowed more pictures in the Poona history. Unfortunately printing in black and white does not do justice to the bright colours (yellow and red) seen at any Poona event!

I am very grateful to many individuals who have helped in the production of the two histories, including:

Harry Anderson
Brian Appleton
Chris Atkins
Lady Henrietta Bennett
Anthony Bridgewater
Martin Claridge
John Evans
Prof Sir Malcolm Green
Belinda Hadden

Alastair Hall
Will Henderson
Peter Hunter
Nicole Johnson
Tony Landamore
Anthony Lunch
Iain Macdonald-Smith
John Millar
Ellen Milner

Robin Nott
Barry Parkin
Prince Philip
Andrew Reid
Graham Self
Jyotsna Shahane
Rob Sherrington
Ed Smith

I would also like to record my grateful thanks to a number of publications and publishers for the material that I have reproduced:

American Sailor Magazine
Anything But Sailing (the history
of West Kirby Sailing Club)
Daily Mail Newspaper
Field Magazine
Guardian Newspaper

Independent Newspaper
Tatler Magazine
Three Chousing Reers! (Reggie
Bennett's memoir)
Times Newspaper
Yachts & Yachting Magazine

Considerable effort has been made to trace copyright holders but if any has been inadvertently overlooked the author will be pleased to make the necessary arrangements at the first opportunity.

75 YEARS OF PORT

THE HISTORY OF THE

OXFORD & CAMBRIDGE SAILING SOCIETY

By Jeremy Atkins

STEWART MORRIS, OBE
(1909-1991)

The following obituary, written by John Barker, appeared in The Independent on 25th March 1991 and is reprinted by kind permission of The Independent, Obituaries.

For years and years Stewart Morris was known and loved, not only by small-boat sailors in the Solent and Chichester Harbour, Torbay, Falmouth and Lowestoft, but in Montreal, Toronto, Annapolis, San Francisco and Vancouver.

Morris was this country's most successful dinghy helmsman, winning the coveted Prince of Wales Cup for the International 14ft class 12 times. He found time, after the sixth of these wins, to compete in the 1948 Olympic Games in Torbay and win the gold medal in his Swallow Class yacht, appropriately called Swift.

He learnt to sail on Hickling Broad, Norfolk, on his father's punt, and there is no doubt that patience necessarily developed in those narrow rivers and broads stood him in good stead later. After leaving Charterhouse he went to Trinity College, Cambridge, and whilst there he helped to form the Cambridge University Cruising Club, of which he was the first President in 1930.

Following his conception and introduction of team racing against Oxford, with three boats on each team, Morris founded the Oxford and Cambridge Sailing Society in 1934, four years after leaving Cambridge. By now the International 14ft dinghy was almost more important than his early business life as a hop-broker in the family firm.

Competing against friends like John Winter and the late Sir Peter Scott, Morris won the Prince of Wales Cup four times between 1932 and 1936, in a different boat each year - each designed and built by the infamous Uffa Fox at his Cowes boatyard. Despite their beautiful construction, Fox built these mahogany-planked boats, with ribs every two inches of their 14 feet, for less than £200, including all the gadgets of the day.

In these pre-war days and especially when sailing in Hayling Island Morris was a local hero. He won all his races by the length of the harbour. Despite his success he was always accessible, especially to the young and always ready to advise. He was especially kind to many "young" New Zealanders when they came to this country to challenge his feats on the water.

Morris liked to win and, as a small boy, I remember watching the Prince of Wales Cup at Falmouth in 1938 when he was beaten by Peter Scott and John Winter sailing their boat Thunder and Lightning using a trapeze harness from the hounds of the mast to keep their boat upright in the strong wind. Morris was furious when Scott and Winter went past him using this new "gadget" and after the race he called a general meeting of the class owners to ban formally the device from any further use; this proposal was carried and the trapeze harness, so widely used in dinghies today, did not appear again in approved racing until 1963.

During the war, Morris joined the RNVR and, after a period in destroyers, his ability to think two-dimensionally was put to good use in aircraft carriers where he became an accomplished fighter direction officer. With three other wartime officers he developed a successful air defence system for the Carrier HMS Formidable in which they were serving at the time and Morris, who was then a Commander, was appointed an OBE.

4

After the war, Morris ordered a new boat from Uffa Fox and it was in his Martlet in 1947 that I crewed for him on several occasions. Morris was methodical and exact, every piece of rope was marked for specific conditions and he invariably sailed the boat exactly upright in all states of wind and sea. He was a marvellous seaman with an excellent eye for the weather, judging it by watching cloud movement and formation.

When racing, whilst he was very difficult to pass on a beat to windward, he had exceptional powers on a reach (sailing at approximately right angles to the wind), where he would get his boat "planing" (with the hull partially out of the water) earlier than anybody else and would streak ahead of the competition. Nowhere was this planing technique more effective, and more necessary, than in winning his Olympic gold medal in 1948. In the seventh and final race of the series, Morris had to be better than fifth to guarantee first place. At the end of the last beat of the race, the Portuguese boat, his chief rival, was leading and Morris was fifth, in light winds, with two reaching legs to go. Suddenly the wind increased and on the reach to the finish, Morris and his crewman Derek Bond got Swift planing and passed the Brazilians to take fourth place and the gold. In the 1950s and 1960s Morris won the Prince of Wales Cup on five occasions, in new boats.

Ashore, Stewart Morris made a tremendous contribution to the success of post-war dinghy sailing as Chairman of the Yacht Racing Association (YRA, later known as the RYA) Dinghy Committee and although he gave up all his committee work at the age of 65, he was recalled to succeed Prince Philip as President of the RYA from 1980 to 1983. During this time he had to rebuild the Association's morale after the non-participation of British yachting teams in the 1980 Olympic Games and he was instrumental in getting the newly formed sport of windsurfing accepted into the RYA's committee structure as he had persuaded the RYA Council to do for motor-yachting in the early 1950s.

THE FORMATION (1934-35)

The first page of the Society's first Minute Book records in Stewart Morris's hand:

Following various discussions between members of the Oxford University Yacht Club and of the Cambridge University Cruising Club, a circular letter was sent out to certain selected members of the two Clubs with the object of discovering whether they were in favour of forming a new club, association or society which would help keep members of the two Clubs together after coming down from the University, and encourage team racing throughout the country, at the same time maintaining a high standard of helmsmanship.

While a carbon copy of the letter is pasted into the Minutes Book, the quality is not sufficiently good to reproduce the original here. The letter, which must have been sent out late in December 1933, read:

Dear Sir,

    It has been decided to form an Oxford and Cambridge Sailing Society with a limited membership drawn from the two Universities.

    The object of the Society is to give its members further opportunity of taking part in team races and to foster this sport in various parts of the country.

    It is intended that the Society shall arrange matches at weekends with most of the principal small boat clubs.

    We suggest that a Committee should be elected at a meeting early in the New Year and, in the meantime, we propose to act as the Committee.

    It is suggested that the subscription should be £1 per annum to defray expenses, the principal of which will be donations to the Prize Funds of those clubs who offer us their hospitality.

    We are writing to you to know whether you are interested in this scheme and willing to take part in it. As the membership will have to be drastically limited we hope to hear from you within a few days.

R.de Quincey
H.F.G. Harrison
P.V. MacKinnon
S.H. Morris.

Writing in 1984, one of the authors of this letter, Roger de Quincey, provided a bit of background to the proposal: *"I remember the British 6 metre team had*

been thrashed by the Americans in the 1932 BA Cup, and some of us felt impelled to learn more about team racing. And so the Society was formed."

The letter was sent to twenty three people. Stewart records in the Minute Book that twenty two signified their intention of giving the scheme their whole-hearted support, while the other, Harry Burke (Cambridge Captain, 1930), refused *"on the ground that he was going abroad shortly, and therefore could not be as active a member as the new club would need, but wished it every success."*

However, his actual letter survives, and in it he expresses a concern that his involvement would be less than Stewart might be looking for:

I very much appreciate being involved in the limited membership. However I get so very little time now for that sort of thing that I am afraid I must refuse the offer as I should only be a passive member and that rather defeats the object of the Society. I am very sorry indeed, but there it is, if I were one of the unemployed I would jump at the offer as it sounds a marvellous scheme, however in present circumstances I think it best to refuse.

Another reply which is preserved is interesting to note, partly because of his role in the ensuing history, but also because of his views on inland sailing. Chris Boardman replied:

The scheme sounds like a good one to me and I should like to take part in it. However, although you have my support as far as I can give it, yet, as you know, my activities are really confined to one Club [the Royal Corinthian Yacht Club at Burnham], *which I have no doubt will do anything to help you with your scheme as far as it is able.*

Anyway, I wish it the best of luck. As far as taking part in the scheme I am not keen on up river racing or rather inland water racing not because I do not enjoy sailing thus, but because I am N.B.G [no bloody good, I assume] *at the finer art now.*

Chris Boardman also said: *"I should like to belong if only to show that the R.C.Y.C. will be prepared to help you in anything you do which concerns team racing and the smaller classes, both of which the R.C.Y.C. intends to encourage as far as possible."* However, as we will see, this was not a view shared by all members of the Burnham club.

On 31st January 1934, a second letter was sent out to the twenty two inviting them to a meeting of the Society which would be held at 6.30pm on Friday 24th February at the Royal Thames Yacht Club in Knightsbridge. The recipients were invited to submit *"any ideas which you think should be incorporated in the provisional rules to be drawn up by the Committee prior to the meeting."*

The fact that the Society's first meeting was scheduled to start at 6.30pm, but actually commenced at 7.45pm, did nothing to avert progress.

Seventeen of the twenty two who replied positively to the original letter were present:

L.A. Biddle	J.F.W. Dilke	S.H. Morris
C.A. Boardman	J.D.C. Ewing	J.D. Russell
J.A. Boycott	H.F.G. Harrison	P.M. Scott
J.H.L Burroughes	C.S. Leaf	T.H. Scott
P.E. Clift	P.V. MacKinnon	G.C. Tozer
R. de Quincey	A.J. Morris	

Absent, but signifying their willingness to join the new Club were:

P. Brett	H.T. Kemsley	Sir J.N. Nicholson Bt
R.G. Cooke	P.M. Munro	H. Trefusis

P.V. (Bee) MacKinnon was elected chair of the meeting and Stewart Morris outlined his scheme:

A Club should be formed, to be called the Oxford and Cambridge Sailing Society, the objects of which should be to encourage team racing and to keep together the cream of the Universities' helmsmen after they 'came down', requiring a high standard in candidates – both of helmsmanship and of personal charm.

The minutes record what sounds like a harmonious meeting, and Stewart's outline was *"agreed to unanimously"*. But the minutes also note that there was *"a considerable amount of criticism and discussion"* as the draft rules for the Club were debated.

Perhaps the first evidence of this was when Chris Boardman criticised the name of the Club, saying that, what was initially recorded in the minutes as *"outsiders"*, but later changed to *"certain people"* from the Royal Corinthian Yacht Club considered it a name to which the persons present had no claim – it would not be representative of either Oxford or Cambridge.

However, Chris Boardman's comments were not received positively – it was pointed out to him that the seventeen members present included twelve past officers of the two University clubs, and that every other proposed member had some claim to be a worthy representative of one or other University club.

Chris Boardman beat a hasty retreat (perhaps worried that he would not be considered to have the high degree of personal charm that Stewart's outline sought!) and said that he was voicing other people's opinions – not his own.

8

The draft rules of the Club were subject to much debate and amendment.

Two significant matters were debated and decided which have set the tone of the Society for many years.

On membership, it was originally proposed that *"The Society shall consist of no more than twenty five members."* However, this was amended to limit the membership to the number decided in General Meeting each year (with twenty five being the number for 1934), *"but the maximum number shall not in any one year be increased by more than six."*

It becomes clear over the years that the latter wording was not as intended – certainly by Stewart, who interpreted it as referring to the number elected each year, rather than the number of members. However, it is perhaps understandable that, in the mid 1930's, recent graduates were only anticipating increases in membership numbers and not thinking that they might be mortal.

On subscriptions, a proposal of a guinea annual membership fee was accepted, but concern over *"possible future financial difficulties"* were solved by adding a rule giving a General Meeting *"the power to raise subscriptions for all members at its discretion."*

It must be considered a credit to the Society that, although discussed from time to time, this power has never been invoked in 75 years and members may continue to pay an annual subscription of one guinea, although most have now opted to pay a larger, one-off, life membership fee.

Some of the suggested changes to the draft rules were less serious, with Bee MacKinnon proposing that: *"The Honorary Secretary shall always be a person who has at some time won the Prince of Wales' Cup."* A rule that, although not officially adopted, was observed for 32 years!

The Society's first set of rules was as follows:

RULES AND REGULATIONS

NAME
1. The name of the Society shall be the Oxford and Cambridge Sailing Society.

OBJECTS
2. The objects of the Society are the encouragement of yacht sailing and racing and – in particular – team racing.

MEMBERSHIP
3. Election of all candidates for membership shall be by the Committee. Every candidate shall be proposed and seconded by members of the Society, to both of whom the candidate shall be personally known.

Both the proposer and seconder shall write letters to the Secretary of the Society in support of the candidate.

Membership shall be confined to present or past members of the Oxford University Yacht Club or of the Cambridge University Cruising Club, who are no longer in residence as undergraduates.

4. The membership shall be limited to such a number as the Society in General Meeting each year decide; but the maximum number shall not in any one year be increased by more than six.

OFFICERS

5. The Officers of the Society shall consist of a President, Honorary Secretary, Honorary Treasurer, and Honorary Deputy Secretary.

COMMITTEE

6. The Committee shall consist of the Officers and two other members. At all meetings three shall form a quorum. When present, the President shall be Chairman, but in his absence a Chairman shall be elected before any business is transacted. At any Meeting, in the event of equal voting, the Chairman shall have the casting vote.

7. It shall be the duty of the Committee to manage the affairs of the Society, subject to the approval of the Society at its General Meeting.

GENERAL MEETING

8. The Officers and Committee shall be elected for one year only by a simple majority of the votes of members present at the General Meeting to be held during February each year.

At a General Meeting, when present, The President shall be Chairman, but in his absence a Chairman shall be elected before any business is transacted.

ALTERATION TO RULES

9. The rules of the Society shall not be altered except by a two thirds majority of members present at the Annual General Meeting or at an Extraordinary General Meeting called for that purpose. At such a Meeting not less than one third of the members of the Society shall form a quorum.

Two weeks' notice shall be given to all members of any proposed changes in the rules.

HONORARY MEMBERSHIP

10. The Committee shall have power to elect any person as an honorary member of the Society for such a period not exceeding one year as they may think fit.

SUBSCRIPTION

11. The Subscription shall be One Guinea per annum payable to the Honorary Treasurer on the 1st January in each year.

12. The Honorary Treasurer shall produce, at the Annual General Meeting, correct accounts for the past year, ending 31st of December in the preceding year.

13. The Society in General Meeting shall have power to raise the subscription for all members at its discretion.

14. The Committee has power at any time to expel any member.

Rule 14 was actually proposed by Chris Boardman "*as the meeting was breaking up*" and "*was carried unanimously*". I suspect neither he, nor anyone present, expected him to propose its use just two weeks later! On that occasion it was not invoked, but it was something regularly threatened to Chris Boardman himself in the 1940s for failing to pay his subscription!

Once the rules and regulations had been agreed, all those present, and the five absent, were elected as the twenty three foundation members of the Society.

The Officers and Committee were also elected:

Hon. Secretary	S.H. Morris
Hon. Deputy Secretary	R. de Quincey
Hon. Treasurer	J.D. Russell
Committee	J.D.C. Ewing
	P.V. MacKinnon

It was decided to leave the post of President vacant until the Club had proved a success.

Stewart Morris had obviously been hard at work because he announced to the meeting that he had provisional promises of six fixtures.

The idea of a dinner was also discussed. This was left to the discretion of the Committee – to be held either late in 1934 or early in 1935, although no record of a formal dinner in these years exists.

Having started an hour and a quarter later than intended, and after much had been discussed, there is no record of when the meeting finished, but it must have been late. At least two members subsequently wrote to Stewart apologising for having left early!

The Fixture List

One of those who left early went to the theatre and had an encounter which clearly worried Stewart and potentially threatened some of his plans. The member, John Boycott, wrote to Stewart the next day about the views of the Royal Corinthian Yacht Club at Burnham:

Dear Stewart

I was so sorry I had to go away last night especially as the show I went to was BUM. However I learnt one thing which is why I am writing. I had to sit next to that flat faced stiff Ogilvie (our Commodore) and happened to mention the Society without indicating that I had any connection with it. He was talking big about the Sharpie fixture list for this year ('matches with all the important small boat sailing clubs in England etc') and said they had heard from you and turned it down on the grounds that you were going round cadging matches and offering nothing in exchange. I said I had heard that you had thought of making the usual sort of contribution to the prize fund and he shut up. I don't suppose it makes any difference but you had better know.

I hope the Society can spare a match v. the Hospitals club; as we have no prize fund it can go on the free list.

Yours ever

John Boycott

Stewart immediately wrote to Chris Boardman, another Royal Corinthian YC member. Sadly we do not have what Stewart wrote, but Chris Boardman's reply stated: "*Most of your letter is nonsense and I can't spend a lot of time answering it in detail.*" However, he continued:

If you heard that some gentlemen had got together and formed themselves into a Club and issued challenges to Clubs to a team race in those Clubs' boats without there being any chance of a return match what would you expect people to think. Everybody does not know yet who the members of the Society are nor what their objects are. I warned you some people would think this – and they do and it is only natural until they know more. The member of the Society who reported this incident to you ought to be the first one to be expelled if he did not do his obvious duty of explaining why the gentleman was mistaken in his views of the Society, instead of being all annoyed because a very reasonable view (in my opinion) was expressed. One of my objects in coming to the meeting was to warn the Society of this and there's no need to be annoyed about it, but there is a need to prove these people are mistaken.

With regard to a match in the Sharpies with the R.C.Y.C., the Flag Officers and Committee including all prominent Sharpie owners would like a match. I have had a chat with all of them and, if the member of the Society

you talk about had done his duty, I should have been saved the trouble of doing mine.

Nevertheless, as I have been put in charge of the doings, I don't feel inclined to offer dates if you feel a match with the R.C.Y.C. wouldn't be thought a good idea by the O&C.S.S.

The Sharpies have got dozens of matches and I don't think the R.C.Y.C. would thank me a lot if it meant me going down on my bended knee on their behalf. They aren't that sort of Club.

Actually, I'm a trifle upset to think that, having been given the job of arranging a match with the R.C.Y.C. by the O&C.S.S., I shouldn't be considered the right man to judge whether the R.C.Y.C. want a match or not. After all I am on the Committee of this Club and I don't think the anonymous member of the O&C.S.S. who talks so much is. However, we'll leave it at that. I'm not really annoyed, but I do think it all a trifle ridiculous but on the whole I think I had better wait to hear from you before I offer any dates.

We hear no further of this matter, but seven fixtures were arranged in the first year. There is no record of these, but by 1935 that list had grown to thirteen. Two of these fixtures involved multiple teams in the same race, but Stewart was no doubt very proud of the performance. Of the sixteen clubs sailed against, the Society beat eleven of them, drew with two and lost to three:

United Hospitals SC	Won 25 – 17
Alexandra YC	Won 23 – 19
Oxford University YC	Won 11 – 9
Royal Norfolk & Suffolk YC	Lost 19 – 22
Royal Mersey YC	Won 19 – 15
Itchenor SC	Won 24 – 18
Island SC	Won 25 – 22 ½
Royal Southern YC	Won 25 – 7
Royal Artillery YC	Won 25 – 14
Eastbourne YC	Lost 20 – 18
North Norfolk SC	Won 11 – 9
Aldeburgh YC	Drawn 20 – 20
Portsmouth Victory Class	Lost 6 – 12
Royal Corinthian YC	Won 25 – 17
Cambridge University CrC	Won 13 – 10
RYA Dinghy Team	Drawn 13 – 13

Of the twenty three founding members of the Society, all but two competed in at least one of these fixtures with, inevitably, Stewart Morris being the most regular attendee at nine of the thirteen.

13

First Committee Meeting

The first Committee Meeting of the Society was held on 9th September 1934 at the Frensham Pond Hotel, with Roger de Quincey, Bee MacKinnon, John Russell and Stewart Morris present.

They elected John Winter as the twenty fourth member of the Society, so, although not a founding member, he was elected in the first year.

The Committee also decided that "*in view of the success the Society had experienced during the Summer*" they would recommend the election of a President in 1935.

Two names were discussed: Sir John Beale and Mr. J.S. Highfield, but "*it was considered that Sir John Beale would in every way be more acceptable to the members.*"

The First Annual General Meeting

Eleven members were present at the First Annual General Meeting of the Society, held on 22nd February 1935 at the Royal Thames Yacht Club.

The first accounts were shown to the meeting and approved. Of the twenty three members, twenty two had paid their guinea. The surplus for the year was 6s 10d, and the Society's Balance Sheet recorded £16 9s 1d.

The Society's first President, Sir John Beale, was duly elected and the existing Committee re-elected.

A description of the flag flown during matches in the previous year was also officially adopted as Rule 3: "*The Flag of the Society shall be a dark blue flag bearing a lion passant gardant or with paw raised on a book gules charged with a cross orb.*" All subsequent rules were re-numbered.

While the Society's idea of proposing team races to clubs in their own boats did, as we have seen, raise some concerns, it is clear that there was a generally positive reaction, as has been seen by the number of fixtures, but also by the fact that the Society's advice was being sought about team racing.

Stewart Morris reported to the meeting "*that some clubs had asked us to give our opinion at the end of a season on the best method of scoring points in team races.*"

GROWTH IN THE PRE-WAR YEARS (1935-40)

Having completed its first year, successful on the water and with some recognition of its potential role in the development of team racing, it looked as if the Society was set for a prosperous future.

Elections To Membership

However, perhaps inevitably, a club which required *"a high standard in candidates - both of helmsmanship and of personal charm"* would generate some debate about potential members.

For both John Winter's election in September 1934 and the next group in 1935, there are no records of letters of proposal or seconding. It appears that the Committee simply agreed on the individuals.

At a Committee Meeting on Friday 22nd February 1935, held at the Royal Thames Yacht Club, it was proposed to recommend to the AGM that the membership for 1935 should be increased by the maximum number of six. If this was adopted, it was agreed that the new members should be:

J.A.F. Beale	R.C. Droop	D.L. Pollock
N.G. Cooke	H.L. Paxton	W. Rendell

Given the membership increase was ratified, these six were duly elected.

However, the Committee's decision was not to the liking of Chris Boardman who wrote to Stewart shortly afterwards:

You may as well know that I want the procedure of elections to the O&C.S.S. altered. ... I want the names of all the candidates for election sent round to each member so that if anyone knows any reason why he doesn't want a certain candidate elected, the Committee can consider his concerns.

Frankly, I object to one of the candidates ... There's no need to tell you why or whom as he's probably elected now but if I'd known sooner I'd have written quite a lot. He's just N.B.G. [again!] in a boat!

For the 1936 elections it appears that things had got more formal and Chris Boardman's proposal followed.

Members were written to, asking for nominations, and letters of proposal and seconding were received. In December 1935 Stewart circulated to members a list of five potential candidates.

One of these candidates provoked a private and confidential letter from John Russell, stating that the individual's election would not be in the interests of the Society because he believed that membership should not be

open to *"persons who have been 'sent down' and been unable to obtain a degree."* Subsequently the proposer and seconder withdrew their nomination.

One other candidate was proposed and seconded after the initial circular. He was not elected and, one suspects, Stewart Morris's views, expressed in a letter to the proposer, held sway:

My own view about him is that, although he is a very nice chap, we do want members who are both competent helmsmen and able to sail and as he lives in Lancashire I do not think he could do the latter. We have quite enough passengers already.

This individual was eventually elected to membership in 1968, some thirty two years later!

Not surprisingly, this is not the last time there was debate about the suitability of certain individuals for membership! But four members were duly elected in February 1936 by the Committee, having given members the opportunity to comment on the candidates and decide on the maximum number of members at the AGM.

Sir John Beale

Having been elected as the Society's first President, Sir John Beale hosted a dinner at the Junior Carlton Club, about which there is a note in the Minute Book, written by Stewart in pencil, who clearly enjoyed recording it:

Note: During the early Spring of 1935 the President, Sir John Beale, gave a memorable dinner to the Society at the Junior Carlton Club after which Roger de Quincey was knocked down in St James' Square by a driverless, locked up, parked car.

Sadly, however, Sir John Beale's tenure as President was short lived – he died in December 1935.

At the second Annual General Meeting (1936) Jack Ewing *"stated what a great loss the Society had incurred by the sad passing of Sir John Beale, the President, who, among his other great qualities, had the wonderful facility of understanding young men, and being regarded by them as a great personal friend."*

It was decided that the office of President should not be filled for 12 months as a mark of respect.

Second Annual General Meeting

But not everything at the second Annual General Meeting was in sombre tone. Towards the end of the minutes the following is recorded:

16

The Secretary [Stewart Morris] *then arrived and the members present, apparently overcome by the bounteous liberality afforded to them made it clear that they wished inserted in these minutes the following statement: "That a message of sympathy and regret be delivered to the Honorary Secretary in view of his misfortunate shipwreck today coupled with congratulations on his merciful preservation by the Almighty from the Perils of the Deep, and an expression of confidence that in any moment of panic onboard he bore himself bravely as befits a member of the Oxford and Cambridge Sailing Society."*

The Honorary Secretary, not having been drinking all evening, could not see the humour of this.

Unfortunately we do not know what this is referring to, but it was clearly something enjoyed by the members, if not by Stewart!

The First Annual Dinner

It would appear that the first formal Annual Dinner was held on 29th February 1936 at the Royal Thames Yacht Club, one week after the AGM. The menu (complete with spelling mistake), signed on the back by those attending, shows they enjoyed a six course meal, but the wines are not listed.

Diner

Huitres
--
Consomme de Volaille
--
Saumon Bouilli, Sauce Hollandaise
Concombre
--
Poularde de Surrey roti
Pommes Chateau
Chouxfleur
--
Peche Melba
--
Canape Baron

29.2.36

Olympics

1936 also saw the first Olympics since the Society had been founded.

The trials were held at Burnham in the summer, and Stewart proudly records that *"over half our members took part"*, and Club members were victorious in two of the four classes - not a bad achievement for a two year old club!

A complete Society crew won the Six Metre class trials, with Chris Boardman helming and Charles Leaf, Mike Bellville and Arthur Morris (Stewart's brother) crewing. Three of these Society members were in the Gold Medal winning crew in the Olympics at Kiel in Germany.

Chris Boardman's success has often been recorded in Society lists of Olympic medal winners, but the records do not usually show that Society members Miles Bellville and Charles Leaf were also part of this gold medal winning crew. (Arthur was, however, replaced by a non-member for the Olympics).

The trials for the single handed class were won by Peter Scott, from Stewart Morris. Peter Scott went on to claim the bronze medal in the Olympics (*"nearly a silver"*, according to Stewart).

Stewart Morris was the team manager for the British team, and Kenneth Preston (who was later elected a member of the Society) competed in the Eight Metre class.

Matches

Perhaps distracted by this Olympic involvement in 1936, the Society's team did not perform so well, winning only one of the nine matches – drawing two and losing six.

The results in 1937 also proved disappointing. Only six were held and half of these were won.

Stewart was clearly frustrated as he indicated in the circular at the end of 1937: *"It has not been a particularly successful season owing to the fact that we had less fixtures than in past years."* He complained of *"lack of support"*. He went on:

Of the races that were sailed, the United Hospitals S.C. was beaten fairly easily and the matches against Itchenor and Cambridge University were won by bare margins. The match against Bembridge was probably the best of the year and this would have been won but for a slight error of judgment on John Dilke's part in tacking too close in front of the man behind him. The Aldeburgh fixture looked like a win until Charles Leaf unfortunately went aground, while the match against Oxford was abandoned owing to a gale which made the question of sailing quite impossible.

It is hoped that next year members will find it possible to take part in more fixtures but I would like some indication of what they will be able to do before I arrange the fixtures as it is a bad thing to arrange a match and then to let the other Club down.

This was further discussed at the Committee Meeting on 22nd December 1937. It was stated that the Secretary would arrange the fixtures, but that he would ask for better support at the General Meeting.

There was also a discussion as to whether, in view of the poor attendance at fixtures, membership should be widened to allow election of undergraduates (if suitable) who have raced for Oxford or Cambridge against the other University. This was raised at the AGM in 1938, but referred back to the Committee, who, perhaps with their minds on other things, decided to do nothing further and dropped the matter.

Things were not much better for the team racing in 1938 – seven fixtures were held, but again only three won, and those were the inland ones against the two Universities and Ranelagh Sailing Club.

Stewart Morris with B T Whinney & Their Fourteen in 1936

Individual Successes

However, individually, Society members performed very well over this period. The Society had its first top three places in the International Fourteen's Prince of Wales' Cup (Stewart Morris, John Winter, Peter Scott) in 1936.

They went one better the following year, with the top four places [Peter Scott, John Winter, Stewart Morris, James Beale]. The only other time the Society has claimed the top three places was nearly thirty years later in 1965 [Stewart Morris, Mike Peacock, Ian Cox]).

1938 saw a Society boat capture the Prince of Wales' Cup for the fifth year in succession (seven years if you count Stewart's two pre-Society wins), in the famous victory by Peter Scott and John Winter using a trapeze for the first time.

Members went on to win nine out of the first ten PoW Cups following its formation. (At the time of writing, the current score is twenty seven Society PoW victories in 75 years, with Stewart Morris winning ten of them!)

Port

The Society's first ownership of port came about through a gift from Charles Leaf of vintage port and brandy in 1936. This consisted of:

> 6 bottles of Dow 1896
> 6 bottles of Croft 1900
> 12 bottles of Taylor 1912
> 12 bottles of Fonseca 1920
> 12 bottles of Tuke Holdsworth 1927
>
> 2 bottles of Club Liqueur Brandy

The wine was stored at Stewart Morris's office cellars at 9 Southwark Street, London. SE1.

Whether as a result of this gift or not, Charles Leaf was approached with a view to becoming President. *"It was felt that no other member of the Club could fill the position as well, for he is both older and more popular than any other member and has shown on many occasions that he has the interests of the Society at heart."* He was duly elected at the Third Annual General Meeting on 12th February 1937.

Later in 1937 the President hosted a cocktail party at the Imperial Hotel, Torquay, during the International Coronation Regatta in July, where the Club was honoured by the presence of HRH the Crown Prince of Norway.

Dinners

The second annual dinner was held at the United University Club on the 26th February 1937, attended by eighteen members – once again a six course meal, but this time we know of the accompanying wines:

Montilla
Rudesheimer 1933
Chateau Margaux 1920
Cockburn's 1912
Cognac 1884 or Armagnac 1888

The members did not get to taste any of Charles Leaf's gift on this occasion. This was drunk for the first time at the dinner in 1938 to which a number of guests were invited "*by way of returning thanks to Clubs which have given us their hospitality*".

Guests attended from Bembridge Sailing Club, Island Sailing Club, Royal Thames Yacht Club, Itchenor Sailing Club, Oxford University Yacht Club and the Q Class.

No details of the 1938 dinner are preserved, but one can only assume it was another six courses!

War Looming

On 20th September 1938, Stewart Morris contacted the members of the Committee by telephone "*in view of the Czechoslovakian Crisis and the possibility of an European War*". This was described as an Informal Committee Meeting (perhaps the first telephone conference call!), and was minuted as follows:

It was agreed to place on record that the Banking account of the Society is at the Westminster Bank Ltd, 47 Moorgate. EC2.

It was also decided that, in the event of the unfortunate decease of the Treasurer, the President, Secretary and Mr. Ewing's signatures should also be valid at the Bank to draw cheques, and a form to this effect was completed. It was arranged that the files and other records should be moved, if necessary, to the President's house in the country.

However, despite these preparations, the Society largely continued as usual. Proposals for membership were requested in early 1939 and five new members were duly elected, with two more later in the year. Interestingly Stewart Morris would appear to have been happy for these seven elections in one year – something he would later describe as "*illegal*"!

The number of fixtures that were held in 1939 again increased by one to eight. There would have been more but "*the later ones were cancelled for obvious reasons*". However the team were more successful than in recent years, winning six of the matches.

Shortly after war was declared on 3rd September 1939, letters were issued to all members stating that no subscriptions were required until further notice.

However, the Treasurer, John Russell, was obviously chastised by Stewart Morris for not returning the 1940 subscriptions to members. Russell replied from H.M.S. Ark Royal in April 1940:

I purposefully forgot to do anything about returning them. I am willing to take all the blame as it seems to me that:
1. *A little extra in the bank does no harm.*
2. *A bird in the hand etc.*
3. *One guinea can't make much difference to most of our members.*
4. *They ought to have dealt with the matter at the time.*
5. *The war will soon be over, and we shall all have to pay for 1940 – I hope.*

In January 1940, Stewart wrote to members with the news that there would be no General Meeting and providing a list of all the members who were now in the services and their rank.

The Society's records were sent to Arthur Morris at Deddington for safe keeping, but the port remained at 9 Southwark Street.

On 9th August 1940 a letter was sent from Stewart Morris's office (he was now onboard H.M.S. Ambuscade) to members stating that £80 had been lent to the Treasury free of interest for the duration of the War. It went on:

He is also very pleased to inform you that, during a conversation between Lieutenant Ewing and H.R.H. The Crown Prince Olaf of Norway, H.R.H. asked whether, as an Oxford man, he could become a member of the Society. His Royal Highness has, therefore, been elected to membership and has very graciously consented to be the Society's Patron. He appreciates that the Society's activities are bound to be dormant during the War but he is anxious to show his interest in the Society.

The Hon. Secretary has also asked me to tell you how very glad he will be to receive letters from members of the Society to let him know, within the bounds of discretion, how and where they are.

Between 1940 and 1944 various sums were invested in Defence Bonds.

RE-BUILDING (1945-48)

As would be expected, members of the Society played a very active part in the war. Stewart listed all the 48 members during this period in the Minute Book.

Most are listed with their military rank, and any decorations, although there are some farmers, and people working in industry (e.g. P. Brett – ICI, Poison Gas Manufacturer). Perhaps the most cryptic occupation is that listed beside the name: Norway, HRH Crown Prince of. It reads *"Busy as such"*!

The Society suffered less than many organisations as a result of the war. As Stewart wrote in the first post-war letter sent to members on 10th December 1945: *"On the whole I suppose we must consider ourselves lucky, particularly since, so far as I know, we have no casualties since 1942."* Stewart recorded the *"position at 31st December 1945"*:

- Casualties: N.G. Cooke (Flt. Lt., D.F.C.) (Dunkirk); D. Wilson (Lt., (E) R.N.V.R.) (HMS Dorsetshire, Ceylon); P.M.Munro (Lt., R.N.V.R.) (Suicide).
- 1 bottle port broken by enemy action.

The Re-Building

Monday 10th December 1945 was clearly the day that the Society's post-war renaissance began in earnest. Not only did Stewart issue the letter to members, but the Committee also met for the first time in nearly six years, at the Royal Thames Yacht Club.

The Committee confirmed H.R.H. Crown Prince of Norway's election and agreed that he would not be asked to pay a subscription.

The Society was in a strong financial position thanks to the generosity of members who continued to pay subscriptions during the War (and John Russell's foresight in not returning them), with total assets of £203 3s 7d. It was decided that the £80 lent to the Treasury for the duration of the War should be reclaimed, and a further £25 was invested in 3% Defence Bonds.

Stewart felt that the Society had an important role to play at this time:

Having amongst us members of so many different clubs and having now five members of the Y.R.A. Council as well, we ought, apart from our actual fixtures, to be in a position to help a great deal towards getting sailing going in this country on a sound basis.

The first formal post war meeting of the Society was held on Friday 15th February 1946 at the Junior Carlton Club. For the first time, the Annual General Meeting and the Annual Dinner were held on the same evening.

However, one has to have some concerns about the effectiveness of the AGM since it was scheduled to be held after the dinner!

Nevertheless, twenty three of the forty five members attended, and the minutes note that the meeting was held "*after / during Dinner*"!

There is no record of the dinner, except the venue and cost (17s 6d), but it would appear that the post-war restrictions meant a move away from the pre-war opulence of six courses with six different wines / spirits being served. Certainly the next dinner we have on record (1948) was only a three course meal, with Alsace Riesling served initially, followed by beer, then port.

Having not had any elections (apart from Prince Olaf) for six years, the members were conscious of the need to bring in new blood. It was decided at the AGM "*to waive the limit of members in Rule 5 for this year ... and to consider a further increase next year ... The Committee to elect such members as it thought fit, having regard to the need of new and young blood, and also the requirement that not too many should be elected in one year.*"

On the subject of fixtures, Stewart "*stressed the need for a sure attendance in this first post-war season, mentioned the difficulties of filling teams at the last moment and asked that we do a few fixtures well to re-establish our reputation.*"

In March 1946 six members were duly elected. Two had been undergraduates well before the war and it was agreed that, "*as a general principle, future members should be young and that older candidates should only be elected if they had either sailed for their University when an undergraduate or had shown especial merit since.*"

Along with replenishing the membership, 1946 was the year when discussion also turned to renewing the port stocks. At a Committee Meeting at the Junior Carlton Club on Trafalgar Day (Monday 21st October) it was agreed that "*enough vintage port should be purchased to provide for the 1947 dinner, and that, if a suitable opportunity should occur, to purchase a larger quantity of a young vintage for future purposes, the Secretary and Treasurer were authorised to procure it, the sum expended not to exceed £50.*"

Six bottles of Martinez 1922 were bought in 1946 at a cost of 30 shillings each, which is the first record of a purchase of port by the Society rather than a gift from a member.

A further six bottles of Fonseca 1927 were purchased in 1948 for £6, followed by seven bottles of Taylors 1912 for 30 shillings each in 1949 (and a bottle of brandy for those who did not like port!). The Society's policy of investing in port had well and truly begun.

The Remembrance – The Loving Cup

In early 1946 Roger Gresham Cooke offered to present a Loving Cup to the Society in memory of the three members who fell in the War (including his

brother). This was formally presented at the AGM in February 1947 and has been used at the Annual Dinner ever since.

The Loving Cup, Presented To The Society By Roger Gresham Cooke, In Memory Of The Three Members Who Died During The War

In the present day, the ritual that accompanies drinking out of this silver chalice is bizarre to new members, but they can rest assured that they are not the first to find this so. Indeed, a note on the subject was circulated to all members, which provides a suitable introduction and explanation even today.

It also illustrates that traditions do not remain the same. Now (and throughout my membership of the Society since the early 1980s) the cup is

filled with champagne and circulated at the end of the meal, but it used to be different, as can be seen below.

THE LOVING CUP

It has been remarked that the introduction of the Loving Cup at the various dinners nearly always starts controversy on the correct procedure amongst those present; it is therefore hoped that the following few lines may be of interest, not only to those who do not attend the dinners regularly, but also to those members who do.

The passing of the Loving Cup filled with spiced wine, immemorially termed sac, is characteristic of many City banquets, and is usually performed by the Gardeners' Company. Immediately after grace the Master drinks a hearty welcome to his visitors, and the following procedure commences:

Upon rising to drink from the Loving Cup, the persons on the left and right of the drinker also stand. The holder of the Loving Cup bows to the neighbour on his left, who removes the cover with his right hand and retains it, whilst the holder of the Loving Cup drinks, applies a napkin to the mouth of the Loving Cup and replaces the cover. Whilst he is doing this his right hand neighbour stands back to back with him, on guard against attack. The cup is then passed to the left and the procedure repeated, so that there are ALWAYS THREE, BUT NEVER MORE THAN THREE, STANDING AT THE SAME TIME, namely, the drinker and his two neighbours, who are pledging his safety.

This interesting old-time procedure, like the glass bottomed beer mug, is a reminder of the ancient days when the act of drinking was sometimes made an occasion for assassinations, in the same way as the underlying idea of removing one's gloves in shaking hands goes back to the time when the assassin's dagger found concealment in his gauntlet.

The Cup was first used at the 1947 dinner which was, once again, held separately from the AGM.

Resumption Of Sailing

Details of the first post-war match were circulated to members by Stewart at the start of the year: *"The first match will take place against Cambridge at Ely on Sunday January 27th, in the new boats, to be followed by a lecture in the evening by Uffa Fox."* But it does not appear that this fixture was held.

However, eight matches were held: against Cambridge (twice), West Riding, Bembridge, Itchenor, the Solent Six Metre Class and the Fife class in the Menai Straits. The Society won half these matches, which Stewart described as *"quite satisfactory ... considering that many of our members have been out of practice."*

Stewart reported: "*The racing in each case has been excellent and we have improved as we have gone along. The hospitality we have received has been excellent.*"

In announcing the Menai Straits match Stewart acknowledged it was a long way to go, but said "*I think it is worthwhile as it will 'spread the gospel' of team racing.*" However, it sounds like this had already been preached in Anglesey – the match report reads: "*Our hosts were very much better than we were and knew their team tactics. They fully deserved their win.*"

Over half the members of the Society sailed in at least one of the fixtures, but the enthusiasm was not sufficient for Stewart: "*I found it quite difficult to raise teams and had to rely on a few stalwarts. I hope that next year, when members have settled down to their civilian occupations again, it may be easier for them to get away to matches more frequently.*"

Stewart was perhaps more satisfied with the individual triumphs of Society members. Peter Scott and John Winter again won the Prince of Wales' Cup for International Fourteens, Roger de Quincey "*won all his 20 sq. metre races in Lowestoft in his new boat ... and David Pollock beat the Star boat champion of the Argentine in a special match at Buenos Aires.*"

1947 saw eight fixtures again, with the Society winning all but one of them. At these, the Society started to present tankards to the host clubs to give as prizes for their club fleet racing. The Society won the Trent Cup and the Ranelagh Team Trophy this year.

The Committee

The President, Charles Leaf sailed in two summer fixtures in 1946, but by October was ill in a Nursing Home. The Times announced in January that there had been a slight improvement in his condition, but by October 1947 the Society was mourning the untimely death of its second President.

Rex Janson was elected the next President in February 1948 although, perhaps in recognition of the effect on previous holders of the post, "*the Committee suggested to him that this should not be regarded as a life appointment but an honour which might be offered to other members from time to time.*" In the end, he resigned in 1952 after four years as President.

But while the Society was getting through Presidents with indecent haste, the Committee had all but stayed static for the first twelve years.

At the Committee Meeting in October 1946 David Pollock proposed that "*it should become a matter of practice for the members of the Committee to be replaced at fairly frequent intervals and that they should not, in the normal course, hold office for more than 3 years. The Secretary was instructed to mention this in his letter calling the General Meeting and to state that the present Committee members did not seek re-election.*"

However, the minutes also record that *"both the Secretary and the Treasurer deplored this suggestion, while approving the principle of not allowing the Committee to become a clique"*, and no mention of it was made in the letter.

Nevertheless, it is recorded at the AGM that *"the Secretary informed the meeting of the decision of the Committee that all the officers and Committee members would be pleased to stand down and make way for younger blood."*

However, every member of the Committee was re-elected, although it was decided to increase the number of ordinary Committee members from two to four, and to elect University Liaison Officers.

The Committee Meeting in October 1946 discussed four candidates whose names had been circulated to members. *"After some discussion"* it was decided to elect only two of these, and *"to defer the election of R.H. Tizard and J.G. Marshall, the latter because he had not been properly seconded."*

John Marshall was present at the 1948 AGM (although his election is not formally recorded), but Dick Tizard had to wait until 1967 to be elected. He is then just in the list of those elected with no comment about the deferral of twenty years. He was immediately elected the Cambridge University Liaison Officer, a role in which he served the Society for eighteen years.

The Olympic Year

1948 started with a well attended AGM and dinner (twenty seven present), held on the same night, at the United University Club for the first time.

But 1948 was a busy year for the Society and, in particular, for its Secretary, Stewart Morris. This may be the reason why no formal meetings were held after February and the minutes of the meetings that were held were very brief, neglecting even to mention who was elected.

Stewart wrote in February that *"owing to the Trials for the Olympic Games, it seems probable that there will be less support for fixtures in the early part of the summer than usual."* Of the five classes in these trials, the Society had representatives in four of them:

- one in the Six Metre Class
- four in the Dragon Class
- two in the Swallow Class
- four in the Firefly Class

Despite the numbers, only one Society member was selected for the Olympics, but he, Stewart Morris, went on to win the Gold in the Swallow class. In addition, two Society members, Peter Scott and John Winter were on the YRA Olympic Committee and Kenneth Preston was a member of the International Jury.

Stewart Morris In Swift at the 1948 Olympics

1948 was one of Stewart's most successful years and he was presented with a cigarette case from members of the Society at the 1949 AGM inscribed:

Stewart

With admiration and affection from the Society
1948
Olympic Games
Prince of Wales Cup
Sir Ralph Gore Cup
Society Matches

COMING OF AGE (1949-55)

By 1949 the Society was well re-established and post war Britain and sailing was settling down to a more typical existence.

Sailing

The Society continued to team race actively around the country, with eight matches in 1949, but only three were won. There is no mention of lack of enthusiasm from the membership, and so we have to assume that Stewart was now more content with the level of involvement from his members.

In the absence of that Stewart started using his annual circular, reporting on the matches, to provide tips to his members:

Most of our matches were fairly close and, in almost every case in which we lost, the result would have been different had one or two major mistakes in ordinary racing tactics not been perpetrated. In particular, there was an epidemic of hitting buoys unnecessarily [requiring a retirement in those days] *and a fairly general failure in most matches to cover the opposition properly.*

Two points which have also become apparent are that it is desirable for all members of the team to know what the score is at any time and how it can be improved and, secondly, that it does not appear to pay for a leading boat to turn back and help its own side unless this difficult manoeuvre is well carried out. I personally tried it twice this season and in each case lost a place.

Other gems from Stewart over the years were:

1950: *Both we, to a limited extent, and our opponents, to a greater extent, suffered in matches from not carrying out the basic principles of team racing, which are to avoid hitting buoys or having to retire for other reasons and to cover one's opponents effectively.*

1952: *Our leading boat in this race managed to put one of its crew ashore so that he could run to the local church and read the Lesson at Evensong without unduly endangering its long lead!*

During this period the Society team generally had about six to eight fixtures against other Clubs, along with matches against the two Universities. But in addition to these, the idea of having team racing events with lots of clubs competing was beginning to take shape.

30

The first of these events that I have found evidence for was held in 1948 by Royal St George YC at Dun Laoghaire, Dublin. A Society team was not present, but the West Kirby team (with Society member, Cyril Clarke, in it) were runners up to the hosts. Fired with enthusiasm, they decided to organise a similar event at their Club the following year – 1949.

This was originally called "The North West Firefly Championships" but was actually the first running of a team racing event which, in 1953, was re-named The Wilson Trophy.

The history of West Kirby Sailing Club by John Millar reports on the initial planning for the event, one of whose founders was Cyril Clarke: *"Support would have to be gained from the Oxford and Cambridge Sailing Society, which was then the most important body sponsoring team racing."*

For the first running of the event, racing in the morning was in the estuary and in the afternoon, at low water, on the lake. The Society team for this event was:

Martin Claridge	Michael Ellison	David Pollock
Philip Clark	Stewart Morris	John Winter

Photos From The First Wilson Trophy In 1949

Sadly they did not win this event, but were runners up to Itchenor SC. However, the Society's performance in the first nine years of this event was unparalleled: four times victorious and three times runners up. Sadly since then the record has not been so good, with only one other placing in the top two (winning in 1964).

Nevertheless, the Society has been one of the most regular teams and many members who have attended subsequent Wilson Trophy events will have some memories rekindled by Stewart's report of the first event:

This was an extremely strenuous week-end's racing in which teams of three from seventeen Clubs took part in a knock-out competition. Our team sailed no less than eight races in the two days. We got through to the final, which had unfortunately to be sailed on a small lake, as the tide had gone out from the Dee estuary, and there was little windward work, which had been our strong point in the earlier rounds. We were, owing to this, bad team tactics

and a fouled buoy, somewhat unexpectedly beaten by a team of the younger generation from the Itchenor Sailing Club, who did not change helmsmen as we did.

The W.K.S.C. put up a great show, providing all the boats and very considerable hospitality.

The Society was runner up the following year (1950), again to Itchenor, and the first victory at this event came in 1951 with a team of:

Martin Claridge	Philip Clark	Bernard Coleman
Stewart Morris	John Winter	Stuart Wilson

Martin Claridge sailed with Stewart in the first three West Kirby events, alternating helming and crewing duties. However, Martin recalls that in the second race of a match against Royal St George, when the Society needed to avoid having last place but were placed 3, 5 and 6 on the last leg, which was a run, *"Stewart announced that we* [in third place] *must hang back, catch the Irish boat* [in fourth] *and let our two get ahead. Seeing the look on my face, he very gently said 'Perhaps I should take the helm for this manoeuvre, if you don't mind.' He did, and the Society won and I shall never forget the look of disbelief on the face of the very good-natured Irishman when he found he was last."*

The 1951 success was repeated the following year, by which time the Barnt Green team racing event had been added to the calendar.

The Society continued to contribute to the development of team racing. Stewart wrote to members in 1952:

The YA [Yachting Association] *Protest Committee is due to make recommendations to the YA Council as to whether any special rules or regulations are required for team racing. As our members probably have more experience than anyone else in the country on this aspect of racing, I would be glad to receive any suggestions which you think might be put forward.*

In the same year, Stewart wrote in his review of the season:

Our season has been about as successful as I had expected, though not up to the very successful standard of pre-war years. This is probably due to the fact that much more team racing is indulged in by other clubs than before the war, with a consequent improvement in their ability, and is, in itself, a proof that what we set out to do in 1934, which was to encourage team racing, is bearing fruit.

And in 1955: "*There is no doubt that more team racing is taking place in the country than ever before and I think we may modestly say we are responsible for most of it, since there was practically none when we started our crusade in 1934.*"

The Society made less of a contribution to the Olympic cause over these years. We could no longer boast half the membership taking part in the trials - in the 1952 trials "only" five members took part, and Kenneth Preston (now a member) won the trials and continued the Society's representation at the Olympics (in the Six Metre class in Helsinki).

The Annual Dinner

The annual dinner was also now a regular feature and, apart from in 1947, the AGM was held on the same evening, departing from the pre-war practise.

Having been held at the Junior Carlton Club in 1946 and 1947, the venue moved to the United University Club, where it was held for seven years from 1948 to 1954, before transferring to the Royal Thames Yacht Club for the Society's twenty first anniversary dinner in 1955.

Oxford & Cambridge Sailing Society
21st Anniversary Dinner

Potted Shrimps
--oOo--

Zeigweiler Chablis
1949

Sole Normande
--oOo--

Cotes de Bourg
1947

Roast Saddle of Lamb
Chateau Potatoes
Garden Peas
--oOo--

Canape Diane
--oOo--

Crofts Port
1922

Coffee.

25th February, 1955.

This was a fairly grand affair, held on Friday 25th February, with forty three members present and several guests from clubs the Society sailed against:

- Sir Geoffrey Taylor, President Cambridge University Cruising Club
- R O Bound, Commodore, Royal Norfolk & Suffolk YC
- Lt Col G R Huddleston, Commodore, Bembridge SC
- Anthony Clementson, Commodore, Barnt Green SC
- Robert Garnham, Hon Secretary, Redwing Class
- T E O Williams, Menai Straits Fife Association
- R L Fortescue, Vice Commodore, University of London SC

Sir Ralph Gore, was due to attend, but caught influenza the day before and missed it.

Stewart reports that "*the dinner was a good one*" and there were no speeches "*as usual*". Some 30 members and guests subsequently went to his flat for a nightcap till 0230.

Cocktail Party

1949 saw the introduction of another annual Society event – the Cocktail Party, held in London in the Autumn, "*enabling those members elected since the war to meet the older members, many of whose only activity was to attend the Dinner.*"

Another innovation was that wives were invited, or more specifically, guests were "*limited to one lady per member*".

The event was held on the first Friday in December at Roger Gresham Cooke's flat, with Mrs Coleman and Russell helping Mrs Cooke with the food.

The cost was 10 shillings a head and forty five members and guests attended. It resulted in a loss of 30 shillings, but was deemed to have been a success and was repeated at the same venue the following year.

Thereafter the event was held successfully at the London homes of a variety of members.

Membership

Throughout this period, the membership increased by four to six a year, generally with recent graduates being elected.

Chris Boardman is recorded in the minutes of Committee meetings since 1946 as having not paid his subscription since the war, despite repeated reminders and chasing. At Committee meeting on 17th October 1949: "*It was decided to leave his name off the list of members until he should find himself in a position to pay, when it is hoped that he would make good all arrears.*"

But Chris Boardman appears to have made amends because Stewart reported in 1952 that "*it was a great joy to see Chris Boardman sailing for us again*".

However, the member whom Chris had suggested be expelled in the Society's first fortnight (without knowing his name), was treated somewhat more leniently. John Boycott wrote a letter of resignation in 1952 but "*the Secretary was instructed to write to him to the effect that, as he was a Founder Member, his resignation would not be accepted and that his subscription would not be expected until he should consider himself to be in a position to resume payment.*"

In 1954 Roger Gresham Cooke became the first, and only, member of the Society to be elected to the House of Commons.

The Committee

The Society's third President resigned in 1952, having served in the post for four years. Jack Ewing was elevated from Deputy Secretary to the post.

After two years, Jack Ewing proposed that the Presidency should be moved around and proposed to resign, but "*it was agreed that this resignation would not be accepted for another year and certain remarks were made about a term of three years being desirable for a President to be able properly to control the Secretary.*" In the end he resigned in 1956 after four years in office.

At the AGM in February 1955, "*John Russell then made a very pretty speech in which he said that he desired to mark the 21ˢᵗ anniversary by a presentation in a form suitable to a Society whose principal activities were team races: for which a cup would be unsuitable. He had therefore, after considerable thought, designed the insignia which he wished to be called the 'Treasurer's Tiller' for wear by the President on such ceremonial occasions as he should choose.*"

This is traditionally worn by the President at the dinner to this day.

At this meeting, the President presented John Russell and Stewart Morris with lighters in recognition of the twenty one years' service they had given the Society as Treasurer and Secretary respectively.

Regalia

Flags were common from the first year of the Society, flown by the team at matches, given to some host Clubs and available to members. But with all this activity, there was demand for other regalia.

In 1953 both a Society tie pin and a tie were made available to members for the first time. The tie was "*of good quality, dark blue, uncreasable silk with three lions only on the wide end; only one will show when worn with a reefer jacket*", and cost 19s 6d.

The Treasurer's Tiller, Presented By John Russell

John Evans wrote, when hearing about this book, that *"the story is probably apocryphal, but in the early days of the Society, when its founder members were all bachelors, the first Society tie is said to have been a little different. It is said that the Cambridge lion on the tie had a red appendage which left no doubt that it was a rampant male lion! Probably as the years passed, wives and girlfriends objected and the current emasculated lion came into use."*

While the story may have developed in the telling, it is clearly based on fact, because later in 1953 the minutes of a Committee Meeting read: *"It was agreed that, when the present stock was exhausted, it might be better to reduce the size of the lion, to make it less obviously rampant and to have only one lion instead of three."* This modified tie became available in 1954.

MATURING INTO ADULTHOOD (1956-66)

Signs of maturing began to emerge now the Society was over twenty one.

Membership

The Society's first actual resignation came about after the first Committee Meeting in its 22nd year (January 1956) received report of a letter of resignation from Hugh Harrison, one of the original four founding members, on the grounds that "*he did no sailing and would make way for a younger member*".

The Secretary replied that his decision was a great blow, his resignation would not increase the number of members that could be elected in one year and that he should reconsider his decision. It was decided that "*if he should remain adamant, he should be removed from the list of members at the end of the year.*"

He later adhered to his desire to resign.

But this first resignation did not stop the continual growth in the Society's membership, with the number of members being increased by vote at the Annual General Meeting each year. At the AGM in 1956 this process took the membership over 100, to 102. An attempt was made to limit the number to 100, but it is minuted that "*the Secretary's wish was finally granted.*"

Candidates continued to have to have formal letters of proposal and seconding, were discussed by the Committee, circulated to members and "*in the absence of adverse comment ... were informed of their election.*" The process of nomination was significantly contributed to by the two University Liaison Officers (posts introduced in 1947), who were usually recently elected graduates who still maintained close links with the University clubs or senior officials of those clubs.

Olympics

Jonathan Janson was selected as a crew in the Dragon for the 1956 Olympics and they went on to win the bronze medal in Australia. Another member, Tom Paxton, had been "*a tower of strength to the team as an official reserve*". Richard Creagh Osborne, elected to membership shortly afterwards, sailed in the Finn class.

Trials were not held for the 1960 Olympics, but the selectors placed a number of members on their short list:

- Richard Creagh-Osborne, Jack Knights and Richard Murray in the Finn

- Mike Peacock and David Court-Hampton in the Flying Dutchman
- Jonathan Janson and Stewart Morris in the Dragon

In the end only Jonathan Janson was selected to sail in Naples, but the Society was still well represented with Sir Kenneth Preston as Team Captain and Richard Creagh-Osborne as Reserve. Peter Scott was Chairman of the International Jury. However no medals were brought home by Society members.

The next Olympics, Tokyo in 1964, was the first time in the Society's existence that it did not have a member competing.

Team Racing

The Society team continued to enjoy weekends team racing around the country. Matches against the two Universities and the Wilson Trophy and Barnt Green events were regular features. Matches against individual clubs varied (usually around 6-8 a year). Throughout most of this period the consistent ones were with Itchenor SC, Royal Norfolk & Suffolk YC at Lowestoft, Norfolk Broads YC, Bembridge SC, Seaview YC and the Fife Class in the Menai Straits. Early on matches were also held against University of London SC (Welsh Harp) and Waldringfield SC, but these died out and were replaced by one against Royal Windermere YC.

Stewart continued to report on each match, with the place of each Society member, in each race, recorded. The hospitality of the host clubs was always generous.

In 1958 Stewart wrote: *"we seem to have the right number of matches because I have had a certain amount of difficulty in raising teams and any more matches would make this rather a burden. We have had some very pleasant racing and although the results were not as successful as in some years in the past, I do not think it really matters if we lose as long as the racing is close and our hosts enjoy it as much as we do."*

By now the host clubs were presented with solid bronze ash trays to use as prizes. This appear to have been well received and described variously as *"splendid"*, *"delightful"*, *"magnificent"*, *"very handsome"* and *"an asset to any drawing room"*!

There was great joy when the Society again won the Wilson Trophy at West Kirby in 1964. Stewart Morris was also elected an honorary member of West Kirby Sailing Club in that year.

This was a good year for Society teams, winning the Island SC Team Trophy, Trent Cup and Walker Trophy in International 14s, and the Nina Wood Team Trophy in Fireflies. The three International 14 trophies were successfully defended the following year.

38

Annual Dinner

After the move back to the Royal Thames YC in Knightsbridge for the twenty first anniversary dinner in 1955, this remained the venue until the Clubhouse was pulled down in 1961. The following year the dinner was held in the Naval & Military Club in Piccadilly, to which the Royal Thames YC had decamped.

The new Royal Thames Clubhouse was ready in time for the 1964 dinner, but, instead, it was held at the House of Commons through the good offices of Roger Gresham Cooke. It returned to the Royal Thames YC for 1965.

For the dinner in 1966, it was agreed that, *"as 11 years had elapsed since we had asked representatives of clubs against whom we sailed, as guests, they should be invited as a regrettable but necessary piece of public relations."*

Guests attended from Royal Norfolk & Suffolk YC, Norfolk Broads YC, Royal Windermere YC, West Kirby SC, Itchenor SC and the Menai Straits Fife Association.

The dinner was traditionally held on the last Friday in February, but in 1959 Paul Clift suggested moving the dinner to mid week so that country members could link it with business meetings in London. But there were strong feelings against this from those who had come from far afield, some even remarking that they hoped the evening would be such as to make any work the next morning quite impossible!

This continued to be a running battle with the Committee receiving an *"annual letter"* from Paul Clift on the subject. In 1961 Sonny Andreae added his voice to Paul Clift's appeal but this was again soundly rejected: *"it was suggested that they should change their way of life rather than that the Society should change its tradition."*

Cocktail Party

The Annual Cocktail Party, continued to be a successful annual event, held in members homes in the Autumn. The location varied, but it was held at John Russell's flat for four years in a row (1955-1958) and David Pollock's flat five times during the 1950s and 60s. The visit there in 1959 was the first time that the date deliberately coincided with the day of the Rugby Varsity Match at Twickenham on Mike Peacock's suggestion. This was very successful and resulted in a record attendance of fifty four.

However, the party continued to grow and a limit of sixty was imposed and there was usually a waiting list. So the event moved out of members' homes and into the London Corinthian SC in 1963 and then the Royal Thames YC from 1965 to 1970, when it reverted back to members' homes because of the cost.

Investments

Despite the annual membership still being just one guinea, the Society's finances were healthy. At the November 1956 Committee Meeting it was minuted: *"The Old Defence Bonds were maturing and were re-invested in the recent issue giving a greater return. It was decided to authorise the Treasurer to invest a further £50 in his name in Premium Bonds, partly on patriotic grounds and partly also in the hope of winning a prize which would enable a monster party to be flung."*

At the AGM in February 1957: *"The Committee was empowered to increase the stock of wine as they should deem it necessary. This was already within their powers, but the members seemed anxious to give their blessing to this alcoholic project."*

At the next Committee meeting (in January 1958) it was decided to invest up to £50 in vintage port, *"some of it to be for short term use and some (of the 1955 vintage) to be laid down to be drunk when most of the present Committee might be unable to enjoy it."*

More serious investment occurred in the 1960s:

- 1962: 4 dozen bottles of Warre 1951
- 1963: 4 dozen bottles of Taylors 1955
- 1965: 5 dozen bottles of Martinez 1955

Committee

Now his "baby" had reached adulthood, Stewart Morris thought it was time to pass on the mantle and, at the Committee Meeting in November 1956 he *"raised the point that he desired to vacate his post as soon as a suitable successor could be found, with the enthusiasm of youth, time available and preferably an office behind him."* But no mention of this is made again for several years and Stewart continued his sterling work.

At the AGM in February 1958 the number of ordinary Committee members (rather than Officers) was increased from four to *"not less than five and no more than eight"*, although the approval of this had to wait till during the dinner when the necessary quorum of a third of members was reached!

Not surprisingly, the following year, the quorum was reduced from one third of members to twenty. At the same time, the rule requiring two of the ordinary Committee Members to stand down each year was introduced.

At the Committee Meeting in October 1961 it was stated that Ian Butler would take over from Stewart as Secretary, but at the next Committee Meeting *"Ian Butler stated categorically that he would be unable to relieve the Secretary while he (Ian) was holding a flag at Itchenor Sailing Club. It was agreed that the Secretary would reluctantly continue."*

John Russell was more successful at handing over his responsibilities and, at the AGM in February 1962, was replaced as Treasurer by John Clay.

The President "*made a very pretty little speech in which he referred to all the work which John had done in an honorary capacity for 27 years since the founding of the Society. Keeping it on a straight course and its finances in an healthy state.*" John Russell was presented with a George II Silver Tankard and a modern silver dish.

Stewart kept up his search for a successor over the following years.

At the October Committee Meeting in 1963 it is recorded: "*He was anxious to give up the Secretaryship, but both Ian Butler and David Hare were unable to take it on at present. David Hare might be willing when he was more established in his present job. It was agreed that Brian Appleton should be asked to take on the job of Match Secretary in collaboration with the Secretary.*"

Then at a Committee Meeting in February 1964 Stewart "*hoped that the Committee would seriously find a successor for him and that he would certainly not function for more than another year.*"

And at the Committee Meeting in October: "*David Hare was asked by the President seriously to consider with Brian Appleton whether he or both could take on the Secretary's job ... David Hare promised to give this matter very serious consideration.*"

In January 1965 "*no relief had been found for the Secretary*", but David Hare was proposed as Deputy Secretary "*in order to be trained for the Secretary's post.*"

This ploy worked because at the Committee Meeting in October 1965 Stewart reported that "*he had at last obtained the agreement of David Hare to take over the Secretaryship.*"

And so, finally, at the AGM, in February 1966 "*The President said that it was with regret that he had accepted the resignation of Stewart Morris as Secretary who, as founder and Secretary, had done so much in his 32 years of office towards the growth of the Society.*"

Stewart was presented with a painting by Edwin Hayes of a cutter of the Royal St George YC in Dublin Bay.

MID-LIFE CRISIS (1966-73)

While Stewart Morris's resignation as Secretary after 32 years was clearly a landmark for the Society, he remained heavily involved, and with great influence, until his death. He remained on the Committee for the rest of his life, although he ceased to attend Committee Meetings regularly in the mid-1980s.

The Finances

While a one guinea membership fee had clearly served the Society well for 32 years, and John Russell and John Clay's careful husbandry meant the Society was financially secure, the mid-1960s saw some concerns rising.

At the Committee Meeting in January 1966 the Treasurer "*reported that the accounts for 1965 presented a less attractive picture than in recent years when there were no printing charges due to the generosity of Simon Tait.*"

For a number of years Simon Tait had printed the handbook at no cost to the Society, but he had moved job and could no longer do this (although a few years later he took back the organising of it at a reduced cost).

There was a discussion about increasing the subscriptions, lowering the standards of handbook, or printing it every other year. The Committee finally agreed to look at cheaper printing costs, but not to lower the standard or print less frequently.

Also, while the dinner was costing 53 shillings per head, members were only being charged £2, and the Cocktail Party was also subsidised. It was decided to raise at AGM the whole problem of inflation and to seek the views of members as to whether they would agree to a more realistic price for the dinner or prefer an increase in the subscription.

A discussion took place at the 1966 AGM on the question of the Club's finances. "*A number of suggestions made included raising the subscription, the cost of dinners, a graduated subscription and a dinner cost dependent on age. In general it was felt that some action was called for and it was left that the Committee would discuss the situation and prepare recommendations for the next meeting.*"

However, at the next Committee meeting in October, the Treasurer reported that the balance at hand compared favourably with the figure of a year ago and it was agreed not necessary to recommend an increase to the subscription.

This therefore appeared to be a brief mid-life crisis, because in January 1967 the Committee agreed to spend "*up to £60 on purchasing wine for the general benefit of members at some future dinners.*" There was further

42

good news when the October Committee Meeting heard that £50 had been won on one of the premium bonds.

But by 1970 there was again a deficit and "*it was agreed that the question of income against expenditure should be carefully monitored. Possible solutions were subscription increase and handbook printing every other year or in a simpler form.*"

But again this appeared short lived. Towards the end of 1971 the new Treasurer, Peter Andreae, reported "*a very satisfactory surplus*" and "*it was agreed that he should invest approximately £100 in port and approximately £200 in securities.*" In the end he invested £140 in port and £160 in securities.

A further £300 was invested in port in 1973, and equilibrium appears to have been fully restored.

Team Racing

But it was not only the finances which were suffering a mid-life crisis.

In the October 1968 Committee Meeting it was noted that "*we did not particularly distinguish ourselves at West Kirby* [knocked out in the first round] *... Jeremy Vines agreed to help raise a strong team for West Kirby.*"

In 1969 the team did better, reaching the semi-finals, losing to Hollingworth SC. However, at the Committee Meeting in October "*Jeremy Vines outlined the difficulties of raising a competitive team for West Kirby amongst members. The Committee confirmed that in order to maintain our competitiveness in this event in particular an Executive Committee consisting of the President, Secretary & Treasurer had authority under Rule 11 to elect to Hon. Membership non-members to act as crews for the event. This was to be restricted to wives or regular crews of members.*"

When Jeremy Vines went to Australia in early 1970 Patrick Gifford took over from him as, what was described as "*captain of the dinghy team*".

After losing in the first round again at West Kirby in 1970 Patrick submitted a memorandum to the Committee on the question of how to remain competitive in dinghy events. This was discussed at the October Committee Meeting:

Following a general but inconclusive discussion it was felt that:
  a) *Hon. temporary membership for crews was undesirable.*
  b) *Possibility of a crew membership was discussed, but again there was dangers of creating "second class membership".*
  c) *We might have to try harder within content of present membership.*

It was left that Patrick Gifford and the Secretary (David Hare) would discuss the matter further. They met for lunch and circulated a questionnaire to

members, primarily establishing their interest in sailing for the Society in a regular dinghy team.

At the AGM in 1971 the Committee said that there was a problem of raising competitive teams for the dinghy events and they were "*considering the possibility of widening membership ... so that we were able to get some good crews.*"

But with Patrick Gifford's departure abroad in 1971, some of the impetus behind this initiative appears to have been lost, although we will return to this subject in the next chapter.

In 1969 a team was also entered into the first ever RYA Team Racing Competition, getting through to the third round. In 1970 and 1971 the team reached the Area Finals.

Meanwhile the other fixtures continued very much as before, mainly against Bembridge, Seaview, Itchenor, Royal Norfolk & Suffolk, Norfolk Broads, Royal Anglesey and Royal Windermere. The bronze ashtrays given as gifts were replaced by a glass tankard in 1973.

Dinner

While the financial and sailing sides of the Club suffered a slight wobble over this period, traditions were still being established. In 1966, for the first time, the Annual Dinner menu consisted of Fillet Sole, Roast Saddle of Lamb and Canape Diane – a menu which lasted into the mid 1970s when the Sole was replaced by Plaice, and the Canape Diane by Devils on Horseback.

Olympics

Another tradition returned, after the lack of a representative at the 1964 Olympics, Iain Macdonald-Smith not only competed in, but also won gold with Rodney Pattison, in the Flying Dutchman, in the 1968 Olympics in Mexico.

Iain Macdonald-Smith returned to the following Olympics in Munich in 1972, but only as reserve. However, Simon Tait kept up the Society's representation, competing in the Dragon class.

RE-STRUCTURED FOR THE FUTURE
(1974-1982)

Having survived the mid-life crisis comparatively unscathed, the next decade saw more re-structuring as the Society came to grips with its role in the new team racing environment.

Initial Reorganisation

While Stewart Morris had been Secretary for 32 years, his successor, David Hare, did not last so long. A work move to Dublin forced his resignation in late 1973. The Deputy Secretary stood in for him till the 1974 AGM, but a re-structuring of roles was agreed.

The role of Deputy Secretary was abandoned and a post of Sailing Secretary introduced. Brian Appleton took over as Secretary and Anthony Butler became Sailing Secretary.

Stewart Morris's time as an ordinary member of the Committee came to an end at the AGM in February 1974, but he was permanently co-opted to the Committee at that meeting. The following year Stewart was appointed a member of the Committee for life.

Dinghy Team Racing

Anthony Butler took on his new role as Sailing Secretary with gusto, introducing a successful Irish Tour (with the help of David Hare, now in Dublin) and even proposing an American tour, although this did not come about.

The team for the major dinghy team racing events was also going to be taken more seriously, with practices held before the Wilson Trophy and the RYA Team Racing Competition.

This created some success, with the 1974 team winning the London Pirates event and the Walker Trophy, and finishing as runners up in the London area finals of the RYA Team Racing Championships – the best result to date in this event. However, although it was reckoned to be a strong team, it was knocked out in the first round of the Wilson Trophy.

The London Pirates event was won again in 1975 and the team reached the quarter finals in the Wilson.

These successes in 1974 and 1975 were significantly helped by the involvement of future Olympians, Phil Crebbin and David Wilkins, but by 1976 their focus was more on the five ring event and the results suffered accordingly. In 1977 the Wilson was reported as *"disastrous for the Society"* despite fielding a strong team.

However 1977 did see an extremely strong Cambridge University team winning the RYA Team Racing Championships and the first appearance of a new Club, Grantchester Flash Sailing Club. Both these events were to have a significant impact on the Society.

Grantchester Flash was formed by Cambridge sailors Will Henderson and Michael Hicks in 1976. Will was unsure whether he would sail for the Cambridge first team, having changed his degree course and having less time available. However, he and Michael still wished to sail in the RYA competition and, with the restriction of only two teams allowed in the event per club, they created the new Club.

However, the Cambridge captain, Chris Atkins, selected Will to sail for the Cambridge team and so the Grantchester Flash team that year was composed of Michael Hicks and non-Cambridge sailors.

In 1978 and 1979 a Society team, largely made up of the 1977 Cambridge team, attended the Wilson. In 1979 they reached the semi-finals which was the Society's best result for many years.

In 1981, things came to a head when Stewart Morris, who had by then been elected President of the RYA, found himself presenting the prizes to the winners of the RYA Team Racing Championships. The three helms of the winning team were all members of the Society, but they were sailing as Grantchester Flash SC.

Stewart wrote to Brian Appleton: *"Are they dissatisfied with the Society? Seems to me almost that they are doing now what some of us did 45 years ago – because they aren't catered for?"*

The matter was raised at the next Committee meeting, which was some what embarrassing since two of the Grantchester helms, Will Henderson and Chris Atkins, were on the Society Committee! The minutes for this meeting record:

There then followed a long discussion regarding Grantchester Flash, a team racing club set up by Cambridge undergraduates with some thirty members. At present three Society members form their main team. It seems clear that the Society is failing its younger members in some way, in not providing the impetus for them to race at all the team racing fixtures available. It was felt that some potential new members were wooed away into other organisations before being invited to join the Society and we should therefore bring forward our election to the end of the Trinity term. Secondly we should circularise members, asking them to contact the Sailing Secretary if they wished to enter specific events.

The senior members of the Committee met for lunch in December 1981 and developed a plan to address this issue. At the next Committee Meeting, in

January 1982, the Secretary outlined their discussions, and the following points were agreed:

1. *A team captain should be appointed for team racing events of a national nature, and where it was important to enter a really competitive team.*
2. *We would still maintain keelboats and dinghy fixtures of a "social" variety, which would continue to be arranged by the Hon. Sailing Secretary.*
3. *The team organised by the team captain should be formed of six Society members whenever possible, but this would not be compulsory and would depend upon circumstances – there should, of course, be at least three Society members as helmsmen.*
4. *The appointment of the team captain should be made by the Committee from a short list of best possible choices, and the election of this person would take place at the new June Committee meeting.*
5. *The appointment should normally be for one year only, but could extend to a second if the captain had been particularly successful and there was no other obvious suitable candidate.*
6. *It was hoped the team would be formed of members from both Universities, but this would depend upon individual sailing ability of those eligible at the time.*
7. *The team captain would be an informal post, but he would be asked to be an ex-officio member of the Committee.*

The newly elected Andrew Hattersley was approached and agreed to take on this role.

Other Matches

During this period the Society's fixtures against clubs continued happily, The stalwarts were Itchenor, Seaview, Royal Norfolk & Suffolk and Norfolk Broads, with Royal Windermere and Royal Anglesey appearing irregularly. But Datchet, in Squibs, and Queen Mary, in Lasers, were introduced for a while.

However, an incident at Beaumaris and issues with the insurance of, and damage to, the boats, prompted a discussion at the Committee meeting in November 1980. *"It was agreed that the Sailing Secretary should draw up a list of procedures for team captains of the Society. This should emphasise that moderation is called for when sailing other people's boats and that winning at all costs was not necessarily correct."*

The subsequent document was accepted by the Committee in January 1981.

DUTIES OF TEAM CAPTAINS

1. *Confirm any required final arrangements with team members. Preliminary organisation will normally have been carried out by the Hon. Sailing Secretary.*

2. *Arrange to bring a trophy and present it to the appropriate person at a suitable moment. Explain that the Society likes to see the trophy given as a prize in a race for owners who have lent their boats for the match. Such a race can normally be combined with a club race.*

3. *Chose the pairings in the team carefully to ensure an even spread of local knowledge, boat experience, weight, and ability. Brief possible 'over keen' team members on the importance of 'gentlemanly' sailing. The home club must enjoy the match if the fixture is to prosper. Society members, especially new members, should also enjoy the match. Keep this in mind when selecting pairings.*

4. *If conditions are in any way extreme, brief the whole team on the importance of avoiding damage. If damage occurs, for any reason whatsoever, ask the helmsman concerned to write to the owner and offer to pay the excess on the insurance claim. Also inform the Hon. Sailing Secretary.*

5. *Write and thank the appropriate person within a week of the match and produce a report for the Hon. Sailing Secretary within a fortnight. The report should indicate pairings, and give individual results where three or fewer races are sailed.*

Membership

While the Committee was reorganised and the team regenerated in the mid-1970s, the process of candidates being proposed and seconded, discussed by the Committee, circulated to the membership and elected if *"no adverse comments were received within a week"* continued in the usual manner.

Much of the effort in proposing candidates was down to the two University Liaison Officers, who, since the 1960s, had been John Burgess for Oxford and Dick Tizard for Cambridge.

In 1975, Dick Tizard, wrote to the Secretary, Brian Appleton: *"As far as I know we do not have a woman member, but there is nothing in the rules to exclude them, and now that women are full members of the Cruising Club (and the O.U.Y.C.) I must ask if it is in order for me to propose one?"* He felt that Ann Simon, captain of the Cambridge ladies team which beat Oxford and won the British Universities' Championships had a very high claim.

Brian replied that he thought the possibility of a woman member would, quite possibly *"arouse strong feelings amongst some members"*, but promised to discuss it at the next Committee Meeting.

The papers circulated prior to that meeting, held in January 1976, clearly communicated the Stewart Morris was not in favour of the proposal. The minutes read: *"The question of Lady members was raised. The Society's rules in no way prohibit their membership and therefore no change was necessary as a result of the Sex Discrimination Act 1975. The criteria for membership are still based on having sailed for either University team or for a distinguished sailing record as a graduate."*

The recent Sex Discrimination Act was probably at the back of the Committee's mind when this rather cryptic minute was recorded. It was explained more fully in a letter to Dick Tizard: *"it was felt that at the moment no lady has fulfilled the criteria for membership – that is either to have sailed in the main Varsity matches or to have a particularly distinguished sailing record in later years outside University sailing."*

While Dick Tizard replied that he was *"very content with the decisions that the Committee has made"*, another member put forward a different suggestion in February 1976.

David Thorpe wrote to Brian Appleton suggesting *"that membership of the OCSS should be open to any Oxford or Cambridge graduate wanting to join."* He continued: *"Elitism, if that is what the proposal system is about, is surely outmoded and unhealthy and not, I would submit, in the best long term interests of the OCSS."*

With the next Committee Meeting some months away, a lengthy correspondence ensued on the matter. Brian Appleton wrote: *"Although I have considerable sympathy with your comments about elitism. I really wonder, however, whether our membership comes into that category. I regard the Society as being simply a team racing club whose members enjoy each others' company because they happen to be like-minded and interested in team racing. If we were to follow your proposals I think it would change the whole character of the Club. This could well be a good thing, but would mean that the Club no longer fulfilled the function for which it was founded."*

The Committee meeting in November 1976 endorsed these views.

However, issues still reverberated about the membership criteria, this time around the election of specialist crews. The first to be proposed was Tony Firkins, a top class crew and one of the members of Cambridge's National Championship winning team in 1977. He was proposed for election in 1978, but the Committee did not pass his name onto the membership.

Tony Firkins was again proposed for election in 1979 but *"it was confirmed by the Committee that those graduates who had only crewed in the Varsity Match were not eligible for membership."*

Despite these restrictions, candidates were proposed for election in increasing numbers. In 1980 the Committee took the bold step of circulating seven names of candidates to the members. This created an angry response from Stewart Morris, describing this as *"highly illegal"*. But, as noted at the

start of this history, his original rules only restricted the number of members increasing by six a year, not the number elected. It was the recent death of one of the first characters in this history, John Boycott, which allowed seven to be put forward now.

However, Stewart Morris raised the matter at the AGM in February 1980 and *"it was agreed that in future new members should be restricted to six."*

The whole issue of candidates and elections was re-visited in 1981 and 1982, connected with the Committee's keenness to avoid other potential "Grantchester Flash-style" start ups and to have a strong Society dinghy team.

The timing of elections was amended in 1982 so that nominations would now be invited in March / April with a view of elections being made in June, just after the candidates have completed their degrees. With this change, the circulation of members with the names of proposed candidates was abandoned, and the elections just made by the Committee.

Dick Tizard, the Cambridge University Liaison Officer, also requested (as he had many times) more formal guidelines on nominations and, in view of the interests of a strong dinghy team, whether crews should be elected.

At the Committee Meeting in June 1982: *"it was pointed out that in much team racing at the present time, helmsmen and crews never changed positions and therefore some people concentrated on crewing only. It was agreed that the Society must still aim towards excellence and that we should therefore elect one or two members well known for their crewing abilities. The President* [Martin Beale] *pointed out that our new team was in need of highly skilled crews (as well as helmsmen) and therefore he was strongly of the opinion that a change in this policy should occur. It was unfortunate that some crews had been neglected in previous years, but felt that these might be picked up as members in the next few years."*

Subsequently at that meeting, Steve Smith, the first "Society crew" was elected. Tony Firkins followed two years later in 1984.

While the criteria for candidates were being made slightly broader, this period also saw the second and third resignations from the Society. David Thorpe resigned in 1979 – due to *"having no time to attend OCSS functions"*. Brian Lapthorn also resigned, in August 1980.

Annual Dinner

The final plank of the re-structuring came about around the dinner, traditionally held on the last Friday in February and, since the twenty first anniversary, at the Royal Thames YC.

Costs at the venue continued to increase, but it was a popular place with the members. In 1982 the Committee enquired of members if they would

like a mid-week dinner, which would be slightly cheaper. At the AGM there were sixteen in favour of mid-week and thirteen in favour of the traditional Friday.

The first mid-week dinner was held on Wednesday 23rd February 1983. Dinners alternated between Fridays and mid-week for sometime after that.

Olympics

Over this period, the Society's representation at the Olympics continued. In 1976, for the Montreal Olympics, Phil Crebbin sailed in the 470 class, finishing sixth, but with the potential to have finished higher, and Iain Macdonald-Smith returned to the full team, helming the Soling.

The British Sailing team's boycott of the 1980 Olympics in Russia might have put paid to the Society's representation, but David Wilkins came up trumps, winning a silver medal in the Flying Dutchman, sailing for Ireland.

Finances

As well as investing in port, the Society now started using this investment to secure its future and well as its pleasure. In 1974 the Treasurer was given license to sell approximately three dozen bottles of port at auction in order to balance stocks. Further sales followed in the 1970s, and members were allowed to buy bottles in 1976. Even after this, the port stocks stood at 29 dozen bottles.

Throughout the 1970s the Treasurer, Peter Andreae, was very active in dealing with the Society's assets, both of the liquid and cash variety. However, it was pointed out at the AGM in 1979 that "*the Hon. Treasurer had shown greater skills in the wine market than in the stock market*"!

At the AGM in 1977 the possibility of an increase in subscription was discussed and it was agreed that an increase to £2 was perfectly reasonable, if the Committee felt it necessary. But at a Committee Meeting, in November 1981: "*Peter Andreae made it clear he would resist any attempt to increase subscriptions whilst he remains as Hon. Treasurer.*"

So some things would not be re-structured!

ONTO THE HALF CENTURY (1982-1990)

Following these various reorganisations, the Society was set to sail on towards its half century in 1984 and beyond.

The Dinghy Team

Andy Hattersley, the first official Dinghy Team Captain, set about his new role with great energy. Matches were held against London, Cambridge, Nottingham and Oxford Universities and Castaways (ex London University) in the first few months and the team set out for West Kirby with high hopes.

They gained a comfortable passage to the second round where they met the previous year's winners, Castaways. In the first leg they finished 1, 2, 6 (with one set of penalty points), but in the second leg, sailed the next day, Castaways finished 1, 2 and so won the match.

Castaways went on to the final, where they were beaten by the Grantchester Flash team, with three Society members helming.

While Andy had no problem selecting the helmsmen, he wrote: "*Finding three crews who were not too heavy, and had sufficient skill and knowledge of team racing proved difficult. An experiment with the Oxford Ladies Team proved disastrous for boat speed, though some success was achieved on the social front in terms of Commemoration Ball invitations.*"

In order to help fund this team (which was just not possible from the annual subscription of one guinea), the membership was consulted in the invitation to the 1983 dinner and at the AGM on the same night. From this "*the consensus appeared to be that these* [subscriptions] *should only be increased to cover administrative expenses but that a request for donations towards team racing should be made.*"

Only two dissenting views were expressed, one of which is worth recording: "*I really do not believe that the OCSS should or need worry about financial support for its teams. I assume the team members are either salaried or with private means and that they are taking part for reasons of their own leisure pursuits as well as the more idealistic 'for the Society'.*"

Nevertheless, an appeal for the Sailing Fund was issued in March 1983. 53 members responded, resulting in annual donations of around £330 and one off donations of £500. This allowed considerable support to the dinghy team and a donation of £200 to an individual member of the British Universities Sailing Association (BUSA) tour of America.

The team reached the quarter finals of the Wilson Trophy in 1983.

The dinghy team sailed regularly throughout the 1980s, both in matches against individual teams and the big team racing events of the time like The Wilson Trophy, The Illingworth Cup, Budworth Pairs, London

Pirates, The Foot Trophy, Royal St George and Barnt Green. No outright victories in these were recorded, but they did manage to win the Coleraine 24 hour race twice in three years (1983 & 1985).

1987 saw another quarter finals reached in the Wilson and semi-finals in the Illingworth Cup. In 1988 the Society dinghy team (now captained by Barry Parkin) recorded its first victory since it was introduced in 1982, winning the new Oxford Magnum Team Racing Event, organised by the OUYC. This victory was repeated in 1989 and 1990.

Also in 1989, the Society secured an invitation to the fourth Triennial International Dinghy Team Regatta for what was described as the "World Championship of Dinghy Team Racing", organised by the Larchmont Yacht Club in New York. This was obtained when the Secretary, Peter Dixon, happened to be flying to Oslo and sat next to a member of the Larchmont Yacht Club.

Barry Parkin, the team captain, reported on the event:

The Club was fortunate enough to get an invite to this, the 4th triennial championships, hosted by the Larchmont Yacht Club, which is about 25 miles north of New York City on Long Island Sound.

The competition was for 16 teams that had travelled from Europe, Canada and New Zealand, as well as the host team and a team from Manhasset Bay Yacht Club on Long Island. The boats used were Inter Club dinghies which are similar to Fireflies in shape but with only a single sail. The competition was for 5 boat teams and was initially run on a league basis to allow the visiting teams to get used to the boats before the final knockout rounds.

In the first round, sailed in breezy conditions, the Society team won all 7 of its matches on the water, including a memorable race with the Manhasset Bay team which we won despite having only 3 finishers to their 5, due to capsizes. We subsequently lost 2 races in the protest room and so finished 3rd in the league and thus qualified for the gold league for the next round.

The gold league included the top 4 teams from each of the first round leagues and was sailed in lighter winds. The Society team again sailed well, with consistent starting tactics, which allowed us to take control of the races up the first beat of the single round triangular course. In this league we won 6 out of 7 races, losing only to the very fast home team. This qualified us for the quarter finals, together with the other top 5 teams from this league and the Dusseldorf Yacht Club team from Germany who had won the silver league.

The racing now became very tense, with four semi-final places at stake from the 6 remaining teams. This led to many protests, with the Germans taking the record, having submitted 17 protests from their 3

morning races on one day! This led to the 2 juries working overtime all afternoon, but not to the Germans progressing any further.

At the end of the quarter final league, 4 teams remained: the hosts, who had now won 19 races without loss, Manhasset Bay Yacht Club, the Royal Canadian Yacht Club and ourselves. For the semi-finals we were drawn against Manhasset Bay Yacht Club who featured helmsmen Steve Benjamin and Gary Knapp on their team. We had beaten this team twice in the windier early rounds and then lost to them in the lighter quarter finals. However, the semi-finals day was light and we lost 3-0 after holding winning combinations at the windward mark in all 3 races.

In the other semi-final, Larchmont maintained their unbeaten record, beating the Canadians 3-0.

We then had a sail-off against the Canadians for third place, which we won with two 1, 2, 3 combinations. In the final, Larchmont Yacht Club won the trophy after a very close 3-2 match with the other American team, Manhasset Bay.

The week long event was superbly and professionally organised both on and off the water and hopefully we will be invited back in 1992 to challenge the domination of the host club team.

Team: Barry Parkin, Peter Kennedy, Graham Robinson, Julian Elwood, Rob Plummer, Richard Southern, Graham Self, Cordelia Eglin, Liz Walker and Chris Gibbs.

In 1990, the team won the plate at the Wilson Trophy, the Oxford Magnum (for the third year in a row) and reached the final at Barnt Green (losing to Grantchester Flash).

Other Matches

Meanwhile Graham Self organised the keel boat fixtures over this period, usually involving Itchenor SC, Royal Norfolk & Suffolk YC, Norfolk Broads YC and the Victory Class in Portsmouth.

Although perhaps not as serious as Stewart Morris's team tips, Graham Self still provided them: "*Among the lessons we may have learned is that Swallows don't sail well with a spinnaker attached to the keel, you need to be reasonably fit to keep up with Flying Fifteen owners in the bar at Lowestoft, and you can't short-tack a White Boat in light wind on Wroxham Broad. Also a fully qualified accountant is required to take charge of the kitty at Portsmouth.*"

Membership Criterion

After so much debate over the previous years, the criterion for membership came up again at a Committee Meeting in June 1983. There it was agreed:

1. *That priority for election of members of the Society should go to outstanding helms and crews who were likely to wish to sail in competitive events.*
2. *The election of other candidates should be dependent not just on their sailing prowess but upon whether they would be expected to support Society functions, both sailing and social.*

But it was also noted that *"Stewart Morris stressed that, in considering new members, we should not necessarily fill the vacancies each year, but should pay great attention to sailing ability."*

The question of Board Sailing was also discussed, but *"the Committee did not feel that this activity was relevant to the purposes of the Society."*

The admission of ladies to membership was again discussed at the AGM in 1984, but *"there was no support for this innovation at the present time."*

Jubilee Dinner & Cocktail Party

The dinner to mark the Club's fiftieth anniversary was held at the Royal Thames YC on Tuesday 28th February 1984. Twenty nine members attended with guests from:

- Oxford University YC
- Cambridge University Cruising Club
- Norfolk Broads YC
- Royal Norfolk & Suffolk YC
- Itchenor SC
- Victory Class

On this occasion, fifty years of tradition was abandoned as the President, David Hare, made a short speech.

At the AGM that preceded this dinner, the thirteen surviving founder members were elected to Honorary Life Membership of the Society.

A special Cocktail Party was also held in 1984 at Mike and Sue Peacock's house in Wimbledon in June. To finish the year there was a dinner at the Royal Norfolk & Suffolk YC to celebrate the 50th anniversary of the match between the two Clubs.

Jubilee Team Racing Event

However, despite these great parties, in many ways, the most significant element of the year was the Invitation Team Racing Event organised for the Society by Chris Pugh and Andrew Hattersley and held at Farmoor Reservoir, Oxford in April 1984.

The report in Yachts & Yachting for the event, and reprinted with their kind permission, reads:

Grantchester Flash emerged the winners by a whisker at the Oxford & Cambridge Sailing Society's 50th anniversary team racing regatta, held at Farmoor on April 7th and 8th. The event was generously sponsored by the Biggs Wall civil engineering company [who were also sponsoring the Oxford University YC's Centenary Year]. *The regatta was a special invitation event with twelve of the top team racing clubs of the British Isles present, including the arch-enemies Grantchester Flash and Nottingham Outlaws.*

Conditions were almost perfect on both days, with a cool, light, northerly wind that only occasionally fell a little flat. The racing took place in Laser 2s assembled for the British Universities championships, and it provided some exciting footage for a video of the event, which will be available in due course from the RYA.

Racing on the Saturday was on an American League basis with two groups of six teams. Grantchester Flash and Nottingham Outlaws emerged as clear winners in their group, losing only one race each. Nottingham, in fact, beat Grantchester, but West Kirby beat Nottingham. Royal St George and Oxford University emerged winners in their group with Oxford having a straight flush of five victories, and St George only losing one race.

The semi-finals were unremarkable, with Grantchester Flash and Nottingham Outlaws powering their way to the final over Oxford University and Royal St George.

The scene was therefore set for a real derby Flash-Outlaws final. The Outlaws had the better start in both races, with Flash determinedly pulling back on the subsequent three beats and four reaches. In the first race Flash were aided by the wind getting lighter on the second beat, and they finished a comfortable 1, 2 and 6, with one green penalty to go ¾ point up. In the second race Outlaws built up a commanding lead on the first beat, partly because Flash started team racing too early and could not quite catch up, finishing 1, 2, 6, with one green penalty. This gave Outlaws a five point lead, so everything hung on a pumping protest. Strong feelings have existed for a long time about this, and while no-one would wish for a final to rest on a protest, it was, perhaps, useful that this issue should come to a head at an event where the emphasis was on fun and celebration, rather than a 'serious' fixture.

In the event, Outlaws received a red penalty of six points for pumping and so Grantchester Flash took the winner's trophy by a single point.

A footnote then reads: "*Since we received this report the situation and results have changed. Nottingham should not have been awarded with a 6 point penalty but a 2 ½ point penalty as was written into the sailing instructions.*

This change means that Nottingham Outlaws were in fact the winners of the event not Grantchester Flash."

The reference to red and green penalties, and protests, all seems rather quaint in today's team racing world, with umpires and on-the-water decisions, but that is how it was.

As mentioned in the article, the event was held immediately preceding the British Universities Championships and this allowed the error in the sailing instructions (a lost protest should have meant 6 points – hence the confusion – but the sailing instructions said 2 ½ points in error) to be identified and corrected before that event.

West Kirby generously donated a bell to mark the Society's fiftieth anniversary. It was later decided that this should become the trophy for the aggregate points winner from the two three-way matches between the Society and two Universities which took place each year, and later as the prize for the Society's intergeneration event.

Team Racing Video & Stewart Morris Interview

The Society's event was professionally filmed and a thirty minute video produced to provide an introduction to team racing which was made available both for purchase and for hire free from the RYA. It was supplied with a written introduction to team racing by Chris Atkins.

In its first year, this video was hired by over fifty clubs and bought by ten – continuing the Society's aims of promoting team racing. The team racing shown in the film looks a bit tame when compared to today's tactics, but it still illustrates some good manoeuvres.

As part of this video, an interview was conducted with Stewart Morris and, given that this history has now reached the Society's fiftieth anniversary, it is perhaps appropriate to record Stewart's reminiscences over the first fifty years:

Team racing was only a local sort of thing – a little club in one place would sail against their neighbours; then we bought in this idea of team racing being fun – it was fun, because we met people in the University match and liked them, and we wanted to sail together instead of against each other. And so we made this Oxford & Cambridge Sailing Society to race and spread this team racing idea around the country and, of course, abroad now.

The first team racing I took part in as a young man was on the Norfolk Broads in the local one design classes – it was a local thing. We then had dinghies – fourteen foot dinghies, the early generation of the present International Fourteen dinghy, and in 1934 I took a team out to Canada and we raced at Toronto.

The tactics have all sharpened up and improved, and people have trained. This year in International 14 dinghies on the south coast [for the International team racing] we had teams from Canada, both sides of the United States, Japan and ourselves. It was very interesting that the Canadians had faster boats, sailed faster, but the British tactics were better because they were polished more. The next week was the Princes of Wales' Cup, the World Championships of the International 14 dinghy class, and the Canadians won that because they weren't having a lot of British mucking them about.

In the very early days you tended to sail as fast as you could round the course, and possibly take somebody just away from a buoy to let somebody in. Now there are delaying tactics. If you've got the first and third boats, the first can drop back on the second, flap his sails and spoil the wind all round the boat, while the third one goes off in another direction and comes out ahead. Then they're first and second.

In the very early days when we raced against some people we would find that they would almost take each other's wind on the run because they were used to doing that at the weekend, forgetting that they were sailing for the same side this time.

Now the whole thing has improved, racing is closer, it's a lot of fun. Providing team racing is done in a friendly way – competitive, yes, beat them if you can – but no dirt, no sharpness, then it's wonderful.

Olympics

Perhaps the most disappointing aspect of the Society's fiftieth anniversary year was the fact that it did not have a representative at the 1984 Olympics in Los Angeles. It easily could have if someone had proposed the Oxford Half Blue (from the 1979 Varsity match), John Maddocks, who crewed the Star.

Equilibrium was restored in 1988 when the Society had its best representation since 1936, with three members sailing in the Flying Dutchman class - Roger Yeoman for Great Britain, David Wilkins and Peter Kennedy for Ireland. Sadly they could not repeat the two medals won in 1936.

Intergeneration Team Racing Event

At the Committee Meeting in January 1988, Roger Boden, the Treasurer, suggested *"a team racing event to be arranged between different OCSS generations. There would be suitable handicaps to compensate for declining agility and the intention of the event, apart from enjoying ourselves, would be to bring as wide a range of OCSS members together and avoid any tendency to ossification."*

This was warmly welcomed by the Committee and taken forward to the AGM the following month where it obtained a similar response.

The first event was run by Jeremy Atkins and Howard Williams in October at Oxford Sailing Club. Teams from each decade from the 1940s to the 1980s competed, with a complex handicapping system designed by Roger Boden which ensured that the older teams only had to have one finisher ahead of a youthful opposition to win the match.

It was declared a great success and agreed to try to make it an annual event.

Robert Plummer soon took over as the main organiser of the event (until he was deported to Aberdeen in 1993), with Jeremy Atkins acting as the race officer. Gareth Pugh took over in 1993 and it has since been run by a variety of people, usually the Dinghy Team Captain.

However, the original gentlemanly conduct at the event was beginning to disappear. Bruce Burnett raised the issue of rules observance at the event which he felt was not universal. It was agreed that a protest committee was not a good idea and it was decided *"to emphasise the friendly nature of the event and the OOD's ability to disqualify both boats if there was a collision."*

The event has been held every year except 2000, attracting more or fewer teams. On-the-water judging has been introduced, and it is now an event taken seriously by the current University teams and recent graduates. However, the handicapping still works in favour of the older generations, who occasionally enjoy a sweet victory against the young turks!

A dinner was held at Mansfield College after the 1995 event, with forty nine people attending. This experiment was repeated for two more years. It will be repeated for the 75th Anniversary year, with the dinner, once again, being in Mansfield College.

Social Activity

The Annual Dinner continued at the Royal Thames with the now established menu, washed down by the Society's port which was described at the 1989 AGM as *"increasing in value at a rate which outstripped consumption!"* In 1991 it was reported that there was sufficient for 16 years at the current rate of imbibing at the Annual Dinner.

The Autumn Cocktail Party, having been fairly nomadic, settled at Ian and Anne Butler's house in 1978 where it remained till 1996, when the house was sold and it moved to other members' houses or flats.

SIGNIFICANT CHANGES (1991-2008)

Having got well into its second half century, the death of its founder saw some fundamental changes made to the Society.

The Founder Dies

Stewart Morris was not at the AGM in March 1988 – the first he had ever missed – due to ill health. He sent a message of best wishes and a telegram was sent to him wishing him well.

He was not to attend another AGM and died in January 1991.

In memory of Stewart Morris the Society presented to Itchenor Sailing Club and the Norfolk Broads Yacht Club trophies for the annual matches against the Society. These were beautiful half models – a Swallow for Itchenor and a White Boat for Wroxham Broad. These were presented to the two Clubs at the Annual Dinner in 1992, and continue to be contested keenly.

The Stewart Morris Trophy, Presented By The Society To Itchenor SC

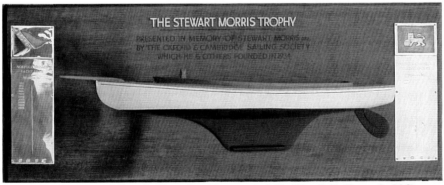

The Stewart Morris Trophy, Presented To Norfolk Broads YC

A Service of Thanksgiving was held on Wednesday 13th March, 1991 in St Paul's Church, Knightsbridge. Ian Butler gave the address, and many Society members were present to give thanks for the person who had given so much to sailing, to team racing and to the Society.

Peter Hunter (not a Society member, but who plays a significant role in the other club featuring in this volume) arranged for the ushers to be composed of Stewart's International Fourteen crews – something which would have been appreciated by Stewart who, in his will, left each of his Prince of Wales' Cup winning crews the replica trophy he had won with them.

As well as the death of the Society's originator, the early 1990s saw three other occurrences which had severe implications on Stewart's foundation.

Financial Crisis Avoided

Just before Stewart's death, the Treasurer, Roger Boden, reported to the Committee an impending financial crisis which threatened one of the constants of the Society – the annual subscription of one guinea.

After over fifty years of free banking, the Nat West bank had unilaterally written to say that they had imposed a charge of 40p per transaction. Clearly this would decimate the value of the one guinea annual subscription.

On telephoning the bank, Roger Boden discovered that the letter's author had subsequently (and appropriately!) been replaced, and the new manager agreed to delay the imposition of the charges for six months.

Roger Boden proposed that, as an alternative to the annual subscription, a suitable life membership fee be introduced. This sum would be invested in index-linked gilts which would give the Society an annual income equivalent to the current guinea subscription. But this would not be compulsory and members would still be free to pay the traditional guinea if they preferred.

This proposal was accepted unanimously at the AGM in March 1991. A year later, 152 of the 220 members had signed up as Life Members and £6,000 worth of index linked gilts purchased.

Membership Criteria Reviewed And Relaxed

While all members have always been welcome to make nominations for membership, this task has mainly been done by the University Liaison Officers. Dick Tizard, as the long standing Cambridge University Liaison Officer (from 1967 to 1985), had frequently requested some clearer criteria for membership on which to base his nominations.

When the author was appointed the Oxford University Liaison Officer in 1990 he felt a similar need and, having been elected Secretary in 1991, took

a more active role in progressing this. I circulated a discussion paper to the Committee in 1991:

OCSS MEMBERSHIP CRITERION

As the OUYC Liaison Officer, and as Secretary who has the responsibility for co-ordinating the nomination and election of new members to the Society, I would like the Committee to discuss the criteria for membership. I feel this is necessary because the current position is not very consistent and has caused some discontent.

I am not looking for detailed criteria to be developed, but for the subject to be aired at a time when we are not considering the election of individuals. I feel this is important because the elections are really controlled by the two University Liaison Officers (their nominations are rarely over-ruled) and to avoid their personal bias (which may be different) influencing the Society they need some input from the rest of the Committee.

Where We Are Now And How We Got There

The Society has always operated on an "exclusive" basis, having only a limited number of members and this would appear to be a very fundamental part of the Club. AGM approval is required to increase the number of members and the constitution states that no more than six members may be elected in any one year.

Obviously to maintain an exclusive club and decide who is to be elected to membership requires some criterion on which nominations and elections are based. The Society's formal criterion for membership is written in the constitution and is very broad, simply being present or past members of the OUYC and CUCrC.

However from the earliest days there has always been an unwritten understanding that only very talented sailors and only men are elected to membership. Talented sailors have, I believe, traditionally been understood to have at least helmed for their University in the Varsity Match and been a regular helm for the University first team.

Up until the mid '70s this worked very satisfactorily because the University first teams usually sailed six helm teams and so those elected were used to sailing both as helmsmen and crews. However, in the late '70's and '80's there has been a dramatic move towards dinghy team racing teams having three helmsmen and three specialist crews. This has applied both to the University teams (for whom the Varsity Match with its six helms is an exception) and the Society's own dinghy team which has been developed more seriously in this time.

In order for the Society's dinghy team to be able to compete against other teams with specialist crews, the Society began to elect to its membership

some individuals who were crews rather than helmsmen. These include the likes of Tony Firkins, Steve Smith and Howard Williams.

At the same time, the OUYC's slightly different structure had given rise to a number of individuals who, although not of the talent level usually associated with Society membership, had contributed greatly to the Club and were considered appropriate for membership. These included the likes of myself, Richard Kendall and Jean Phillipe Snelling.

How Justified Are These Recent Developments
The idea of electing specialist crews to allow our dinghy team to compete effectively clearly is not working. The team captain's brief states that Society members should be picked if at all possible. However, in the 1990 Dinghy Team Report, only three of the eleven crewing places went to Society members. Of the remaining eight places, seven went to female crews. Clearly the captain has felt that these female non-members have given the Society team a better chance than any male members. The results seem to support this.

Realistically, for this to work we would need to elect far more specialist crews than we currently do (and female ones by the look of it!). Should we accept that the Society team is just a Society helmed team?

The election of a limited number of "good chaps" who may not be fantastic sailors may be justified if the Committee feel such people are worthwhile as members, but it would certainly be helpful to have some guidance on this matter (since the Liaison Officer is usually the only one who actually makes this judgement).

What I Would Appreciate Views On
I would be grateful if the next Committee Meeting could consider this matter with a view to providing assistance to the University Liaison Officers in coming up with nominations.

Specific items that views would be appreciated on are:
1. *Should the main criterion for election be sailing talent?*
2. *Should this include crewing talent as well as helming talent (whether to boost the Society Team or not)?*
3. *Should we make exceptions with regard to people who have contributed in a major way to the OUYC, CUCrC or yachting in general?*
4. *Should we actively exclude females?*

This was discussed at the Committee Meeting in January 1992 and there was agreement "*that the Society's current eligibility rules were admirably simple and should be maintained. The Committee felt that sailing talent should be the main criteria for election and that this included crewing as well as helming*

talent. In addition it was generally felt that occasional exceptions to this criteria should be permitted in the cases of individuals who had made major contributions to the sport (either at University or since then) and who would make worthwhile members of the Society.

The Committee unanimously felt that the above criteria should be applied regardless of gender. There was no restriction in the Society's rules by sex and this should be true of proposals for membership.

The Committee then discussed the principle of the membership limit. The maximum number of members could only be increased at an AGM and only by six a year. In practice, the limit was generally increased to enable the election of a maximum of 6 members each year.

The Committee generally felt that a degree of exclusivity was desirable and the usual practise of increasing the membership by no more than six each year was correct. However, in view of the Committee's decision to consider women for membership, it may mean that there is a slight backlog of suitable candidates. The Committee therefore proposed to increase the membership limit at the AGM by six and consider electing more than six members if there were sufficient suitably talented individuals put forward and free membership places.

The Committee was conscious that the nomination of women to membership was reversing a fifty seven year precedent and this might not be welcomed by all the membership. It was therefore decided that the membership should be asked to comment on the Committee's views at the AGM, having been notified of them in advance."

A document was circulated to members prior to the AGM, outlining the situation, detailing the above minute and asking for comments.

At the meeting, in March 1992, the President introduced the topic of the Society's Membership Criterion by saying that no nominations for women had ever been received. However the Committee had reviewed the rules and found that there was no restrictions on membership by sex. They therefore felt it would be right to consider proposals for membership of both sexes.

Dick Tizard quickly corrected the President, saying that he had nominated a female candidate twelve years previously, only to be told by the Committee that the time was not appropriate for such proposals. He was delighted that the current Committee felt that the time was now right.

Ian Butler pointed out that, had members been aware of the lack of restrictions on gender, there would have been more nominations. He said that we were all aware that Stewart Morris would have opposed this move, however Ian said that he wholeheartedly supported the Committee's view.

There followed a series of other contributions from members, all supporting the Committee's view. The Secretary had also received eleven letters about the proposal, ten of which were in favour.

The one which was against was from founding member Paul Clift who said that the 57 year precedent had worked well and he didn't see any reason to reverse it. He added: "*I doubt Stewart would have voted for it, so this seems to me a particularly inappropriate time to raise the issue.*"

But this was the only dissenting voice and, as a result, the Committee had seventeen nominations to discuss at their Committee Meeting in June 1992. The Committee decided to use all ten places available to them, and, of these, half were given to women. A further four women were elected the following year.

While the mention of individual elections has been kept to a minimum in this history, it is worth noting the election of the most senior lady member, Bess Barry (nee Tomlinson).

Bess was at Oxford in the late 1940s and was "*undoubtedly the best Oxford helmswoman of that era*" according to her seconder, Martin Claridge. She had sailed in the Itchenor team that beat the Society to win the first West Kirby team racing event in 1949, alternating as helm and crew (although this is in contradiction to Stewart Morris's report quoted earlier). She did the same with Ian Butler to win the Sir Ralph Gore Cup at the Firefly Nationals in 1948 (alternating with Ian Butler but, according to Ian, "*she sailed all the important windward legs!*").

Martin Claridge wrote: "*I have absolutely no doubt that had Stewart conceived the idea of women members back in the Forties he would have certainly chosen Bess and probably no other woman from either University at the time.*"

The other women who were elected "retrospectively" in 1992 had all won National Championships, been in the BUSA Ladies team or had significant Olympic campaigns.

So, while, in electing women, the Society was almost certainly acting against Stewart's wishes, it was maintaining his standards in terms of the calibre required.

The election of women saw rapid movement in the relationships between members. In the first group of elections in 1992 we gained our first married couple in Simon and Penny Belcher. The following year was the first Society wedding involving John Gilmore and Heather McDowell, and the first father and daughter membership also came about in 1993 when Miranda Merron was elected, joining her father Ken.

While gender equality was a significant change, less than ten years later there were further significant changes afoot.

In 2001, Ed Smith undertook a review of the Society's rules. This was largely a tidying up exercise, but it did include the significant removal of the restriction that the number of members could only be increased by six a year. This was approved by the AGM with apparently little discussion.

While the election of women to membership would not have received Stewart's approval, it is likely that this latest change would have met with even greater disdain, with its implications of watering down the sailing standards required for membership.

This certainly opened the floodgates – in January 2002 twelve people were nominated and seven elected, with a further three added in July.

In subsequent years there have been elections at both of the two Committee Meetings a year, rather than them being decided only once a year as had hitherto been the case. Double digit elections became common place, with thirteen being elected in 2003, and eleven in 2007.

While not connected, it is interesting to note that David Thorpe, who had resigned his membership following a discussion about the elitism of the Society, was invited to re-apply for membership in 2003 and re-joined.

Perhaps as an attempt to avoid a complete free-for-all, Andrew Reid, the Treasurer, wrote a paper about membership criteria in 2001, which was discussed by the Committee at their meeting in January 2002.

No reaction is recorded, but subsequent Committees have used this paper as a basis for evaluating nominations since then.

O&CSS ELECTION TO MEMBERSHIP - SOME THOUGHTS

PRELIMINARY
Objects: *"The objects of the Society are the encouragement of yacht sailing and racing and, in particular, team racing."*

Membership: *"shall be confined to present or past members of the OUYC and CUCrC."*

Guidelines endorsed by 1992 AGM: *"The Committee felt that sailing talent should be the main criteria for election and that included crewing as well as helming talent. In addition it was generally felt that exceptions to this criteria should be permitted in the cases of individuals who had made a major contribution to the sport (either at University or since then) and who would make worthwhile members of the Society."*

DEVELOPMENTS
The Society was formed by Stewart Morris and colleagues in 1934, presumably to mirror similar old boys societies such as the O&C Golfing Society. There was little change until Stewart ceased to take an active role in early-1980s.

At this point the assumption was that if you were a Blue, you would probably be elected. On the basis of six per team (all helming), and an expectation of three leaving each year, led us to the six new members a year.

Of my Varsity Matches all participants were elected immediately or shortly after coming down.

Note that there are many precedents of elections some time after leaving the Universities (eg Standley Bushell, Mark Heseltine).

There have been subsequent developments:
- *Recognition that specialist crews should qualify (Tony Firkins 1985).*
- *A move to nine-person teams (for three-man keelboats) with the third not helming.*
- *Improvement of Ladies sailing, with Ladies elected from 1992.*
- *BUSA increasing in importance vs the Varsity Match.*

Thus the potential pool to be considered each year is no longer twelve; it is perhaps up to forty.

DISCUSSION
The Society should not displace or duplicate Life Membership of the OUYC and CUCrC. It should have a different purpose.

AMR opines that its primary purpose is twofold:
- *racing: to keep competitive teams together after leaving the Universities.*
- *social: for those who have competed with and against each other at Varsity and other tournaments.*

It is therefore subtly different from the "love of sailing" aspects of the OUYC and CUCrC.

ELECTIONS
Whatever criteria are adopted, it is clear that some eligible candidates are missed, forgotten, or not revisited in carry-forward cases. In addition there are those who excel outside after University who are perhaps not picked up.

I opine that there should be a degree of exclusiveness (the inclusive aspects continue through the OUYC/CUCrC) determined through sailing skills.

The spectrum of qualifying criteria (open to restrictive) is:
1. *All past members of OUYC and CUCrC*
2. *have [once] sailed in a University team (first, seconds, men, ladies, helm or crew)*
3. *have [once] sailed in a University first team in any match (helm or crew, men, ladies)*
4. *have sailed in a Varsity Match or BUSA (helm or crew, men, ladies)*

5. *have a full or half-blue (helm or crew, men, ladies)*
6. *have particular skills/talents*

CRITERIA
The Committee would like guidelines to apply to each candidate. The Henderson "Itchenor Jetty" test is a good one other than for specialist crews. Subject to being a "good sort" (without going to Stewart Morris extremes) I suggest:

Category	Presumption	Comment
▪ Captains	Elect	Men and Ladies
▪ First team helm and Blue	Elect	
▪ First team helm - BUSA	Elect	
▪ First team crew and Blue	Balanced	Consider on merits
▪ Specialist crew	Not elect	Consider on merits
▪ Second team	Not elect	
▪ Outside racing success (say top 5 of a serious class)	Elect, if also active OUYC/CUCrC member	
▪ Subsequent success/contribution	Consider	Remember Society's team-racing emphasis

In addition we should have non-binding guidelines on timing. I suggest that once the candidate has come down, that will be OK, except that post-graduates remaining at the Universities (as opposed to joining as a post-graduate) are eligible. There should be an active search to ensure that long-departed candidates are identified.

Andrew Reid
June 2001

Problems With Port

Stewart left the Society £500 in his will, stipulating that it be used "*for wines for the dinner, a cigar box or any other purpose*".

The Committee decided to lay down port with this legacy. However, before this could be actioned, the Society's investment in port was soon to be at risk.

At the Committee Meeting in January 1993 the Treasurer reported that Ellis Son & Vidler, who stored the Society's port, had gone into administrative receivership. 49 of the Society's 163 bottles had been

recovered but there was some doubt as to whether the other bottles would be recovered even though they could clearly be identified.

This was because Ellis & Vidler had followed the standard industry practice of labelling blocks of wine rather than individual bottles – and the receivers were not sure they could accept such labelling as proof of ownership.

Eventually, over the course of several months, and sometimes a bottle at a time, the Society's port was identified and released to it. By August 1994 all but one bottle had been returned. At that stage, the Society's port stocks stood at 145 bottles (some had been consumed during the year).

Once this had been recovered, two cases of the 1983 vintage were purchased with Stewart Morris's legacy.

The Society's port was then stored at Trapps Cellars (and valued at around £5,500). However, lightening struck twice when, in October 2002 Trapps Cellars went into Administration. On this occasion the risk was adjudged to be low because the Society stock was duty paid, clearly marked and packed.

In March 2003 the port was released and moved to Smith and Taylor's cellar in Battersea.

In 2005, the Society received a legacy of £1,000 from Mike Peacock which was invested in 1997 and 2003 port vintages.

Annual Dinner

The Annual Dinner continued to be held at the Royal Thames Yacht Club in Knightsbridge, with the menu being the traditional Goujons of Plaice, Roast Saddle of Lamb and Devils on Horseback (as it had been, with only minor changes, since 1966).

In 1993, the Committee felt that alternative, cheaper, venues should be considered in 1994. However, this was firmly rejected by the 1993 AGM.

Nevertheless the Committee continued to consider various venues in the late 1990s, but none were found or felt to be suitable. However, around this time, and certainly by 1998, the Committee had rung the changes by offering members a different menu at the Royal Thames YC.

But numbers were declining, and hit a low point when only nineteen members were present in 2003. More effort was put in to encourage attendance which reached thirty five the following year.

After much discussion, the break from the Royal Thames YC finally happened in 2007 when the annual dinner moved to the Naval Club in Mayfair. This innovation was repeated the following year.

However, while changes to the menu and venue may have occurred, the tradition that remains is consuming some of the Society's excellent

vintage port – in 2007 we enjoyed the Quinta do Noval 1970 vintage. Of this, Stewart Morris would have approved!

Dinghy Team Racing

Following on from Barry Parkin's successful leadership, the Society's dinghy team continued to compete in a series of events and matches over this period, led by a number of different captains. Major victories evaded the team, but some successes were wins at:

- The London Six Pack in 1999 and 2004
- The London Duck in 2006

Also in 2006, the team came third in the National Team Racing Championships – its best ever result at this event.

However, pride of place has to go to the Society's Ladies team. They first won the Women's National Team Racing Championships in 1994, losing just one race all weekend. This has subsequently been followed by a remarkable succession of victories in 2004, 2005, 2007 and 2008!

This period also saw, despite the Larchmont Event's title, the introduction of the first ISAF (International Sailing Federation) approved Team Racing World Championships. This was hosted by our old friends, West Kirby, in August 1995.

The Society team competed in the Wilson Trophy which preceded the Worlds, getting to the quarter finals. However, there was one Society representative in the first Team Racing World Championships – Amanda Powell, whose team finished sixth.

Since then the Society has been well represented at this event, failing to have a member competing only once, in 1999 – although a Society member did coach a GBR team then, and there has been strong representation of members as coaches and umpires throughout. The full honours list is:

- 1995, West Kirby: Amanda Powell finished 6th. Chris Atkins coached the gold medal winning team.
- 1998, Miami: Ed Smith, Dan Quinn and Chris Lynham won silver. Chris Atkins and Nick Ross were team managers.
- 1999, Ireland: Nick Ross coached the bronze winning team.
- 2001, Czech Republic: Rob Sherrington sailed in the team which finished 5th (two other members of this team were later elected to the Society).
- 2003, New Zealand: Rob Sherrington and the now elected Richard Guy sailed again, winning silver. Chris Atkins was Chief Umpire.
- 2005, Newport: Rob Sherrington again sailed, winning bronze. Chris Atkins was again Chief Umpire.

- 2007, Spain: Another of the 2001 team who had since been elected to the Society, Tom Hebbert, took silver.

Keel Boat Fixtures

At the start of this period the Society's regular keel boat fixtures were down to four – Itchenor SC (Swallows), Royal Norfolk & Suffolk YC (Dragons), Norfolk Broads YC (White Boats) and Portsmouth SC (Victory's).

The Victory match was first to go and then Royal Norfolk & Suffolk. It looked like the Norfolk Broads match was going the same way when it wasn't held in 2001 or 2002, but Tony Landamore helped resurrect it in 2003 and it has been held since.

The Itchenor match has continued to be well supported.

Olympics

The Society was absent from the 1992 Olympics in Barcelona, but returned for the next two events through two individuals.

Ian Walker won silver in Atlanta in 1996 as a crew in the 470 and then went on to win silver again, four years later, in Sydney, this time at the helm of a Star. Barry Parkin also competed in these two Olympics, crewing in a Soling, coming fourth in 1996.

Ian Walker has continued to do great things as a professional sailor, leading the GBR Challenge for America's Cup and reaching the Quarter Finals in the Louis Vuitton Cup in November 2002. At the time of writing, he is skippering 'Green Dragon' in the Volvo Round the World Race.

He was also at the Athens Olympics in 2004, but this time as a coach to the gold winning "three blondes in a boat" in the Yngling class.

Sadly, however, there were no Society representatives actually sailing either in 2004 or in 2008 in Beijing. For the latter, Lizzie Vickers got close in the trials for the Laser Radial Class, but even having a Society member (Chris Atkins) as Chairman of the GBR Olympic Selection Committee was not enough to get her the place!

While there must be disappointment at this lack of Society sailors in the two most recent Olympics, it has to be said that the record for its first 75 years is impressive: there have been 17 Olympics since the Society was founded and members have competed in 12 of them, winning three gold medals, three silvers and two bronze. Quite an achievement for a club which has had less than 400 members in total in its 75 years!

However, it is interesting to note that, of the 20 occasions when Society members have competed at the Olympics, 18 of them were from Cambridge, and only two from Oxford. (Please note that, since the author is from Oxford, this is not a piece of Tab one-upmanship, just an observation on the facts!).

71

LOOKING TO THE FUTURE

Our history has ended, with a review of our members' performances in the Olympics and the World Team Racing Championships. These are ones of which any club would be proud. Combined with our Ladies team's recent domination of the Women's National Team Racing Championships, and a pretty amazing Prince of Wales' Cup record, they make pretty impressive reading.

Furthermore, the work that the Society did in its first few decades to promote team racing helped lay the foundations for the development of this branch of the sport which, in the end, led to the World Team Racing Championships and a Women's National Team Racing Championships.

It certainly looks as if the original aims to *"encourage team racing throughout the country, at the same time maintaining a high standard of helmsmanship"* have been well met. Stewart Morris would have been justifiably proud.

He would probably be less pleased that the main Society team has not had any major victories since the 1960s, but this is something that has been reflected in most sports. While Oxbridge sportsmen used to be at the top of their national games, this is much less the case now.

So where does leave the Oxford & Cambridge Sailing Society?

One person who tried to figure this out was Tony Bridgewater who wrote to members in late 2001, shortly after being elected President, wanting to hear their views.

Oct 2001

An Open Letter To All OCSS Members

I have been meaning to write this note for some months – ever since I was accorded the undeserved honour of being elected President for 2001-2.

First of all, this is my chance to greet all Society members, some of whom I may not have met for many years, or even at all. Secondly, as the OCSS enters its eighth decade, I would like to take the opportunity to hear members' views on the role of the Society and how they see its future.

As you all know, Society activities fall into two categories, Team Racing and Social. Society team racing comprises a limited number of events, usually in dinghies, such as the Wilson and Foot Trophies, as well as the Generation event at Oxford in October (yes, I was there, even if no one saw me!). Keelboat matches consist of the popular Itchenor event in June and the Norfolk weekend in September, as well as occasional matches elsewhere.

Our social activities are centred around the traditional Cocktail Party in December and the Annual Dinner in March (42 Members attended in

2001). This year, in addition, a very successful summer evening garden party was held at the Green's. All these events were held in London.

Most new members continue to be drawn from those who have represented Oxbridge at sailing at the highest level (ie Varsity Match, BUSA etc), by the usual process of nomination and election, although there have always been exceptions.

I would very much like to invite Members to comment on the Society and its activities, and to offer criticism or suggestion on how matters might be changed or improved in the future. Perhaps we've got the model just right. I would like to hear your views. Possible areas to think about:-

- ***Team racing*** *- more, less or different? What about the Generation event (only 5 teams this year)?*
- ***Social events*** *- should the traditional format continue? (I, for one, hope that Julie and Malcolm will repeat the summer party).*
- ***New members*** *- should we aim for a more objective or inclusive procedure? What about the many expert sailors who have slipped through the net?*
- ***Communications*** *- would members prefer more or less information about Society activities and the achievements, sailing or otherwise, of eminent Members? Is the annual address list OK?*

Please feel free to phone or write / e-mail me with any comments or suggestions. To coin a cliché, it is your Society.

I look forward to seeing you at our forthcoming events.

Tony Bridgewater

President, Oxford and Cambridge Sailing Society

The fact that only eight of the Society's 270 members responded to this letter could be seen as either an exhibition of apathy or a demonstration that the Society was currently fulfilling its members' requirements!

The contents of the responses received suggested the latter: "*I believe the current balance is about right*". "*The Society has got the model about right*".

At the following AGM, members expressed the view that the Society was fulfilling the role they wanted from it quite well.

Long may that continue!

SOCIETY OFFICERS

President

Feb 1935 – Dec 1935	Sir John Beale	Feb 1983 – Feb 1985	David Hare
Feb 1937 – Oct 1947	Charles Leaf	Feb 1985 – Feb 1987	Brian Appleton
Feb 1948 – Feb 1952	Captain Rex Janson	Feb 1987 – Mar 1989	Mike Peacock
		Mar 1989 – Mar 1991	John Thompson
Feb 1952 – Feb 1956	Jack Ewing	Mar 1991 – Mar 1993	Peter Dixon
Feb 1956 – Feb 1959	John Russell	Mar 1993 – Mar 1995	Roger Boden
Feb 1959 – Feb 1962	Bee MacKinnon	Mar 1995 – Mar 1997	Anthony Lunch
Feb 1962 – Feb 1965	David Pollock	Mar 1997 – Mar 1999	Richard Heseltine
Feb 1965 – Feb 1968	Graham Mitchell		
Feb 1968 – Feb 1970	Stewart Morris	Mar 1999 – Mar 2001	Malcolm Green
Feb 1970 – Feb 1973	Paul Clift	Mar 2001 – Mar 2003	Tony Bridgewater
Feb 1973 – Feb 1975	John Clay		
Feb 1975 – Feb 1977	Sir Cyril Clarke	Mar 2003 – Mar 2005	Iain Macdonald-Smith
Feb 1977 – Apr 1979	Ian Butler		
Apr 1979 – Feb 1981	Sam Horner	Mar 2005 – Mar 2007	Will Henderson
Feb 1981 – Feb 1983	Martin Beale	Mar 2007 -	Andrew Reid

Secretary

Feb 1934 – Feb 1966	Stewart Morris	Mar 1995 – Mar 2000	Anita Campion / Masding
Feb 1966 – Feb 1974	David Hare		
Feb 1974 – Feb 1983	Brian Appleton	Jul 2000 – Mar 2003	Helen Kerr
Feb 1983 – Mar 1991	Peter Dixon	Mar 2003 -	Tony Bridgewater
Mar 1991 – Mar 1995	Jeremy Atkins		

Treasurer

Feb 1934 – Feb 1962	John Russell	Mar 1993 – Mar 2003	Andrew Reid
Feb 1962 – Feb 1971	John Clay	Mar 2003 – Mar 2006	Chris Fox
Feb 1971 – Feb 1984	Peter Andreae	Mar 2006 -	Nikki Catt
Feb 1984 – Mar 1993	Roger Boden		

Deputy Secretary

Feb 1934 – Feb 1939	Roger de Quincey	Feb 1955 – Feb 1959	Bee MacKinnon
		Feb 1959 – Feb 1964	Ian Butler
Feb 1939 – Feb 1952	Jack Ewing	Feb 1964 – Feb 1965	Brian Appleton
Feb 1952 – Feb 1955	Bernard Coleman	Feb 1965 – Feb 1966	David Hare
		Feb 1966 – Feb 1974	John Faircloth

Sailing Secretary

Feb 1974 – Feb 1985	Anthony Butler	Mar 1992 – Mar 1998	Bruce Burnett
Feb 1985 – Mar 1992	Graham Self	Mar 1998 – Mar 2004	James Skellorn